NIKKI HASKELL'S

☆ STAR ☆
DIET

NIKKI HASKELL'S

☆ STAR ☆
DIET

Nikki Haskell

KENSINGTON BOOKS
http://www.kensingtonbooks.com

KENSINGTON BOOKS are published by

Kensington Publishing Corp.
850 Third Avenue
New York, NY 10022

Library of Congress Card Catalog Number: 97-076119
ISBN 1-57566-283-3

StarCaps,® StarSuckers,® StarBlend,™ StarRoles,™ NikkiBars™ are trademarks of Balanced Health Products. All rights reserved.

First Printing: May, 1998
10   9   8   7   6   5   4   3   2   1

Printed in the United States of America

I am dedicating this book to my mother, Irene,
who told me to live out my dreams,
but always in high heels.

CONTENTS

Acknowledgments   ix

Introduction: Why I Wrote This Book for You   xi

Chapter 1.   The Diet Trap   1

Chapter 2.   Eating Right: Learn How to Eat, Not How
             to Diet   11

Chapter 3.   Labels—And I don't Mean Armani   31

Chapter 4.   Rub a Toad's Stomach and Other Diet Myths   39

Chapter 5.   The Star Diet: Seven Days to a New
             and Better You   51

Chapter 6.   Eating on the Road Is a Piece of Cake   81

Chapter 7.   Star Light, Star Bright, What Do I Eat Tonight?   105

Chapter 8.   All Stressed Up and Nowhere to Go   163

Chapter 9.   Move It and Lose It   175

Chapter 10. StarCaps®: The Celebrity Secret   195

Chapter 11. I Look Greate . . . I Feel Great . . . So Where's
             the Party?   203

Appendix I.   The Star Diet Calorie Counter   229

Appendix II.   Create Your Own Star Diet Diary   247

Appendix III. A Fun Glossary of Foods Your Mother Never
               Told You About   259

Appendix IV.   Metric Conversion Charts   285

ACKNOWLEDGMENTS

I want to thank all the people who have helped make this book possible. Jeffrey Lane who guided me through the rough spots and Richard Hack who helped me focus on the book.

To my wonderful family Ron, Carolyn, Ryan, and Chandler Golbus.

Many thanks to the great photographer, Harry Langdon who made this book cover possible and Michael Hollingsworth, who gave it the "look." Thanks to Tristan Paris and Ann Marso for the makeup, Nick Chavez and Shan Mullis, my dear friends who are responsible for my hair, and Artin for the beautiful jewelry.

A special thanks to Margaux Levy, my cousin and attorney (and her darling daughter Tammy), who is always the backbone of everything I do. I could not have done this without her.

To the saviors, Patricia Harper M.S., R.D., (dietitian *extraordinaire*) and Charlene Rainey (Nutrition Network), whose help and guidance made this book possible.

To my dear friend and close associate, Marc Ritchken, for all the years that he has stuck by me through thick and thin.

To my trusted staff, Gloria Ramirez, Robert Castaneda, and her sisters Nora and Olga, who have all been supportive of all my projects.

To all my wonderful friends Ivana Trump, Beverly Johnson, Suzanne Pleshette and Tommy Gallagher, Lovee and Bob Arum, Robert Evans, Charles Evans, Dennis Basso, Gustavo Novoa, Traci Bingham, Prince Egon Von Furstenberg, Gary Pudney, Jack Martin, Allan Carr, Alan Nevins, Baron and Baroness Ricky and Sandra Di Portanova, Joan Schnitzer, Joan Rivers, Joan Collins, Tommy Corcoran, Lorna

Luft, Jack Gilardi, Stanley London, Mel and Fran Harris, Jill St. John and Robert Wagner, Arlene Walsh, Sugar Rautbord, Vivien and Richard Weisman, Samuel Botero, Neil and Leba Sedaka, Peter Max, LeRoy Neiman, and Oscar De La Hoya.

And to everyone who gave me insight along the way—thank you from the bottom of my heart.

INTRODUCTION

Why I Wrote This Book for You

Here I am with Joan Collins, Suzanne Pleshette, and Connie Stevens at a Christmas Party for Joan.

For the past fifteen years, I have been a pioneer in the diet and health industry. People from all over the world have followed my weight loss plan successfully. For years, the success of my diet had been one of the best-kept secrets of the top stars in Hollywood. My famous friends have begged me to write this book to share the details of the Star Diet System with the world. It has worked for them, and it will work for you.

I developed this diet out of necessity. I have always been diet obsessed. When I was a little girl, I lived in Chicago and was a champion horseback rider. I took a lot of dance classes and ice skating lessons, so at a very early age I got a lot of exercise. At age thirteen I moved to Los Angeles with my family and soon I had put on 10 pounds. That was my rude awakening. I have kept my eye on the diet issue ever since.

As time went on, I became more and more involved in the world of glamor and high fashion. Looking good was not only important, but essential to success. Weight control was vital to me and to everyone around me.

Diet, diet, diet was all I ever thought about. I hoped that someone would come up with the magic answer. No one did. I understand how frustrating the whole diet syndrome can be. It is the single hardest thing to conquer. You would think by now, with all we know, that everyone would be able to maintain the right weight. The truth of the matter is that in the past ten years, the U.S. population has gained 25 percent more weight. Depressing, but true.

I, like you, have tried every diet, read every book, and used every product. None of them work. The information is misleading, and none of the products even live up to their claims. I would lose a few pounds and then gain it right back, and then some. After intensely researching diet and weight loss, through trial and error, I created the Star Diet. Some of the most famous and glamorous people in the world have found this program to be the answer.

The Star Diet will give you the tools you need to lose weight and, most important of all, keep it off. You can finally get control of your life. For the first time, you can be slim, trim, feel good and have fun doing it.

Remember: You don't have to be a star to look like one. You have nothing to lose but weight!

CHAPTER ONE

The Diet Trap

The toughest part of a diet isn't watching what you eat. It's watching what your friends eat."

Robert Stack and me at a fabulous birthday party.

Celebrating with Leroy Neiman, Neil Sedaka at Ivana's.

I t's New Year's Day. You wake up after a great night of eating, drinking, and partying. You say this is the time for me to make my New Year's resolutions. At the top of your list is "go on a diet at once." You go out and buy every new book and article on dieting. You say, "This is it."

If excuses were dollars, you'd be a millionaire. You'll start on Monday, or after you break up with your lover, or when you change your job, or take a trip, or when the kids go to camp. But you still can't button your favorite dress or tuxedo. It's out of control. Instead of having to lose 10 pounds, it's more like 20 to 50. You're losing the diet war fast and it's getting on your nerves. Everyone's giving you that "it's time to go on a diet" look. So you give it a little try. You cut back on bread for 2 days. Nothing. You start to exercise. But you have no direction. It's a little of this, a little of that. Nothing happens, and worst of all, your scale shows ten pounds too many no matter how many times you reset it!

It's now several months later and you've been zoned out, blood-typed to death, matched your food, dialed your meals, joined a gym, sweated to the oldies, spoken to dozens of trainers and nutritionists, and bought gallons of liquid meal replacements. You have more Bun Busters®, Ab Rollers®, and TreadMills® than a gym and guess what? You still haven't lost a pound.

You've watched dozens of shows where everyone is thin. You think no one has your problems? Think again—there are 8 people who look like supermodels and 52 million who don't. In the United

States, 1 out of every two women is on a diet and 1 out of every 4 men. So, you've got plenty of company!

Millions of women have bought into the idea that they should have the bodies of hollow-eyed waifs before they can venture out of their living rooms, and almost as many men think they have to look like pumped-up hunks before they can accompany them. As society's concern with the perfect body has developed into a national obsession, the trickle-down effect has been devastating. Children as young as eight or nine are beginning to restrict their caloric intake or sign up for weight-training programs, and the early signs of eating disorders are showing up in second graders. The resulting epidemic of anorexia, bulimia, and compulsive overeating has reached tragic proportions. Even those who don't fall prey to the more serious disorders end up in a yo-yo cycle of weight loss and gain that can last a lifetime.

I should know. I've done it myself. Boy, have I done it. You don't have to be sitting home alone to become obsessed with your body image. People judge you by the way you look. It's not fair but it's true. If you want to start a business, get a top job, or start a new career, you've got to look your best. But it's not easy. If it was, Oprah would have simply melted away 10 years ago instead of hiring a cook and a trainer and entering 10K runs. If it were that easy, the diet industry in America wouldn't be raking in 33 billion dollars a year while Americans have put on 25 percent more weight. Dieting is one of the things people do most in America, but with the least success. We can learn to fly an airplane, rollerblade, play golf, tennis, or ski, but we can't seem to control our weight.

Living in New York and Beverly Hills as I do, I am surrounded by people who make their living by keeping up their appearance. This is a double-edged sword for me. On the one hand, being surrounded by the most beautiful people in the world is a constant reminder to strive for new heights. On the other hand, I've had access to the stars (they always work the hardest because the camera puts on 10 pounds), their friends, their lifestyle, and of course, their diets. Unfortunately, though, what worked for my celebrity friends didn't work for me.

Jack Nicolson and Robert DeNiro bulked up on huge amounts of vegetables and high-fat steaks. They also work out nearly every free minute of the day, even between takes on the set. Whitney Houston also works out an hour and a half a day, drinks an abundance of water, and eats low-cal meals. Healthy enough, but an hour and a half of gut-busting exercise a day is not my idea of a good time. Dolly Parton swears by the multiple meal approach. She eats twelve minuscule meals a day. Effective, but not very practical for most of us. Neither is hiring a full-time personal chef to monitor everything you eat the way Oprah does. I'd rather have someone take me dancing than hire a personal chef. If I'm going to spend the money, I'd rather go out to a nice restaurant and enjoy what I eat. I order the right foods and always leave the leftovers with the waiter. That way, there's nothing lurking in my refrigerator late at night.

Loni Anderson swears by pasta and fresh fish. Cher, with the body I always wanted to have, maintains by combining a killer workout with a low-carbohydrate, high-protein regimen that excludes pasta and includes a truly foul-tasting tea said to be brewed of gotu kola and dong quai. Only Cher and monks who've sworn to mortify the flesh seem able to swallow the stuff. My idol Elizabeth Taylor, bless her heart, uses a method I can relate to. She likes to hunt and peck. What that means to her is that if she sees it, she eats it. Her solution is to keep food out of sight as much as possible. I know how she feels. Of course, after one day on a starvation diet, any ice cream in the refrigerator starts calling out to me in the middle of the night. Instead of handsome Italians, I find myself dreaming of Ben and Jerry. Out of sight isn't always out of mind.

There are as many get-thin plans as there are stars to promote them, and over the years I tried every one of their approaches short of hiring someone to hound me day and night saying, "Don't touch that!" and taking the cookies out of my mouth. I flung myself body and soul into every sure-fire diet that came along. There was the Banana Diet: two bananas, three times a day. Even a monkey couldn't stay on it. The Beverly Hills Diet was a variation. I consumed more fruit in a day than Carmen Miranda wore in a month. Then there was the Scarsdale Diet, which should have been Jean Harris's legal defense when she shot the doctor who thought it up. For a while I went on the Water Diet, which cleverly sought to substitute water for food in hopes that my body wouldn't notice, and then on the Stillman Diet, which caused me to *gain* weight. The hands-down winner for most disgusting regimen was the Pregnant Woman's Urine Diet. A doctor gave me daily shots of a pregnant woman's urine and a long list of things I couldn't eat. I did lose weight, but on the other hand, I couldn't sit down after a dozen injections in my shrinking tush. I learned in a hurry that the minute you go off a crash diet, you gain 10 pounds overnight.

And then, of course, there was my personal favorite. I simply stopped eating for a while. It's endorsed by every thin woman I know who has a fast metabolism. Dozens of kind friends simply look at you wide-eyed and say, "If you want to lose weight, you should simply stop eating. It's easy." You look back at them and say, "Gee, thanks for sharing. I would never have thought of that. Who knew?" I was never successful at fasting. For me, meals are an integral part of my day—they're fun. I get up at six in the morning and work hard. I look forward to lunch or dinner with a friend or business associate. Buying food from diet centers to cook in a microwave oven really turns me off.

And what was the result of all this effort? My weight dropped; my weight rose. My clothes fit; then they didn't. I was trapped in a yo-yo cycle, and with every new diet I tried, I became more obsessed with my weight. Every time my weight rose, so did my frustration. What made my dietary failures even more irritating was the success I was experiencing in other parts of my life.

I've always been a pioneer, an innovator. I was one of the first eight female stockbrokers in the world in the days when women weren't even allowed on Wall Street, let alone the restaurants on Wall Street. But I would be on the telephone taking an overseas order for a million shares of stock and put the client on hold and go weigh myself. After twelve years on Wall Street, I decided to make a change.

I was the first to start a celebrity talk show on cable. I traveled around the world with the famous and beautiful as part of *The Nikki Haskell Show*. I traveled to the Cannes Film Festival, where I did the last interview with Peter Sellers from the Hotel Du Cap and joined Imelda Marcos and President Marcos at the Philippine Film Festival and danced in the Samba School at Carnival in Rio de Janeiro.

I formed a company called New York Entertainment that created special events worldwide. I helped launch famous discos and clubs like Studio 54, The Underground, Le Club, and Magique. I was living the kind of life most people only dream of—Including me!

None of this, however, relieved my obsession with dieting. No matter where I went, I was accompanied by my image in the mirror and companions with perfect bodies. If anything, my obsession with my weight grew worse. It wasn't until I decided to research weight control myself that I finally found the answer I'd been looking for. I finally had the common sense to study the human body myself and find a weight-management system that really worked. I learned how our bodies actually work: how various foods are digested, how exercise contributes to overall fitness, and how nutritional supplements can aid in this process. The result was StarCaps and the Star Diet; a workable, easy-to-follow plan that actually works. The result for me personally was that I was finally able to maintain the weight I'd always longed for without starving myself, binging on trendy or unfamiliar foods, or working out for hours each day. This approach has worked for me for 15 years. It's worked for my friends, too, and for hundreds of thousands of dieters from all over the world. Presidents to princesses, movie stars to athletes have successfully followed the Star Diet and StarCaps system. I feel it is my responsibility to share it with those of you still trapped in the same cycle that once controlled my life and might control yours.

Before we get started with the specifics, though, I want to make one thing clear. There is no easy, magical way to lose weight and stay thin. The pounds are not going to simply melt away like butter on a summer afternoon. The determination has to come from within you. I recommend that before you begin, you see a physician for a checkup to make sure you have no major health complications.

It is possible to lose weight and keep it off, and stay healthy in the process. To do it, you will need the right balance of food, activity, nutritional supplements, and stress management. Before you panic and think, "What's different about that?" let me give you a few words of encouragement. First of all, nobody starves on my diet. You can eat a remarkable variety of food; the key is knowing which foods to choose. Second, you don't have to work out with Cher or Stallone to raise your metabolism to a decent level. As for the dietary supplements, that's where StarCaps come in. If I do say so myself—and I do!—my personal blend of safe and natural ingredients is a breakthrough in weight loss supplements.

My philosophy for stress management is that it isn't possible to have too much fun, so learn to treat yourself to a good time as often as you possibly can. Finally, and perhaps most important, the Star Diet is intended for imperfect people. It is not a tightrope where one slip means failure. There is no such thing as a perfect dieter, and if there were, you wouldn't want to know them anyway. If you slip occasionally (and you will), learn from your mistakes. We all make mistakes, but we each make them differently. Learning your personal pitfalls is the key to success. A mistake is an opportunity for you to learn something important about yourself. Use that mistake to turn your failure into a triumph. I did, and you can, too.

There are some basic lessons all dieters have to learn, however, and it's time for you to start learning them. So here they are:

★ **1. Stop thinking of a diet as something restrictive.** If you think constantly about what you can't eat, you will be obsessed about it, feel deprived, and will surely fail. Instead think about what you *can* eat. Think in terms of allowance, not in terms of denial. Your diet isn't what you can't eat; your diet is what you *do* eat. This is your new way of eating not dieting. The goal is to learn how to eat so that you don't have to diet forever. Eating right should be a pleasure, not a punishment.

★ **2. Keep a food diary.** We all have convenient memories when it comes to food intake; the only way you will really know what you're eating each day is to write it down. Keep track of every morsel that goes into your mouth, and tally up the calories at the end of the day. This is essential. You'll find it's remarkably easy once you acquire the habit—and more fun than you think.

★ **3. Don't skip meals.** The old "just stop eating" advice will doom you to failure. Regularity in your food intake is the key to maintaining a constant flow of energy.

★ **4. Keep those liquids coming.** Six to eight 8-ounce glasses of water a day are ideal, but if you can't force yourself to drink that much water, you can substitute other noncaloric, nonalcoholic, and noncaffeinated beverages. Caffeinated drinks are not an acceptable alternative since caffeine is a diuretic. Alcoholic beverages are too high in calories. Be careful with caffeine-free diet sodas as well. While they do count toward your daily liquid intake, they contain a high amount of phosphoric acid, which can leach calcium from your bones.

★ **5. Don't give up.** I can give you the tools, but I can't make you use them. No one can go on a diet for you. You have to take responsibility for yourself. On the other hand, taking charge also means that you have the power to change your body into the slimmer, more attractive one you've always longed for.

Ready? Then read on. You'll discover the thin you in the next few chapters. Good luck!

CHAPTER TWO

Eating Right: Learn How to Eat, Not How to Diet

"If it melts in your mouth, it sticks to your hips."

Scott Downie/Celebrity Photo Agency

Left: At Spago's with George Hamilton and Ivana.
Below: With Jill St. John, Robert Wagner.

The key to your success in weight management is understanding what the different types of foods do to your body. Proteins and carbohydrates are the good guys. Carbohydrates are processed quickly and provide an immediate source of energy for the muscles and organs. Anyone who has ever gone on one of those no-carbohydrate diets for long knows what happens to your quick energy: it simply evaporates. Protein, on the other hand, is digested more slowly, to give the body a longer-term fuel. Proteins in particular and carbohydrates to a lesser extent are far less likely to be stored as fat, unless eaten in large quantities.

Fats, on the other hand, are a completely different story. In the melodrama of life, fat is the villain. Instead of burning up in our metabolism, the fat we eat is stored in the body as guess what—fat. This might be all right if we lived in the Arctic or chased down our game on foot, as our ancestors did. There was a time when that stored fat served a useful purpose. But in today's world, where we're more likely to chase a bus than an antelope, and our days are spent in well-heated rooms, all that fat has nothing to do but pile up. And pile up it does.

Unfortunately, the fact that our bodies no longer need large amounts of fat doesn't mean that we no longer want it. On the contrary, our bodies are programmed to crave it. Worse yet, research has shown that the more fat you store, the more you want. It's our body's way of showing us who's boss.

No one is saying it will be easy, but the benefits of cutting back on your fat consumption are so obvious that even the least motivated dieter will be excited by the results. Better yet, as you lose stored body fat, your desire for fatty foods will diminish. If heavy bodies make us crave fat, losing weight helps to lessen the craving. You'll never lose interest in fatty foods completely, but as your body adapts, you'll require less fat to feel satisfied.

Meanwhile, there are plenty of good foods for Star Dieters to fill up on. The first of these is the dieter's best friend: the complex carbohydrate.

Complex carbohydrates. These are nature's wonder foods. Vegetables, grains, and legumes fall into this group. Though most people read the phrase "complex carbohydrate" and hear "carbohydrate," the operative word here is "complex." The complex carbs are not only low in calories; they are quickly processed into energy for that rush of well-being we all love.

One key to complex carbohydrates' wonderful nutritional efficiency is fiber. Complex carbs are all from the plant family. Plant matter has fiber in every cell wall. Animal cells, on the other hand, contain none at all. As you probably know, fiber is a key factor in keeping the intestines clean. That's why it's the key ingredient in every natural laxative on the market. But a clean digestive tract is only the beginning.

Scientists tell us that it takes a good twenty minutes for the brain to signal the stomach that it's full. That's one of the reasons we overeat and don't realize it until it's too late. But because fiber takes longer to chew than most foods, our bodies have time to receive the signal that we've eaten. Complex carbs help our appetites catch up with our bodies. The great joy of fiber for the dieter, in other words, is that it makes you feel full.

As fiber enters the stomach, it expands, giving the sensation that you've eaten more than you actually have. And since the body doesn't digest fiber, it adds no calories of its own. Instead it heads straight to your intestines. As an added bonus, fiber inhibits the body's production of insulin, an appetite stimulator.

Nature has given us a cornucopia of foods rich in fiber. Of all the foods in this category, vegetables are the foot soldiers. Vegetables are perhaps the single most important source of fiber in our diets, low in calories, high in nutrition. They are widely available, inexpensive, and colorful, adding beauty to the food we eat. There is a wide assortment to choose from, and you can choose freely, with very few exceptions. Except for olives, seeds, and nuts, all of which are laden with fatty oil, you can eat as much vegetables you want. Steam, microwave, or bake them to preserve their mineral content. You can even stir-fry them in an oil-free, nonstick pan.

Another wonderful source of fiber are whole grains, whose bran layer has been left intact instead of processed away by manufacturers. In addition to the bran, the germ—the heart of the seed—is an excellent source of vitamins and minerals. As with vegetables, there are many whole grains to choose from. You don't have to limit yourself to bran flakes. Whole-grain pastas and brown rice are excellent sources of whole-grain nutrition. So is bulgur, a grain used in Middle Eastern tabobuleh salad.

The most obvious whole-grain product is bread, but here you have to be careful. Some whole-grain breads have added fat and hidden sugars, so read the labels very carefully before adding whole-grain bread to your diet. Be especially wary of commercial "wheat bread," which is usually just processed refined wheat flour with food coloring added. Look for the word "whole" before the grain to ensure the benefit of fiber. Generally speaking, Star Dieters should limit themselves to one slice of whole-grain bread a day.

In the legume family, beans, peas, and lentils all win top fiber honors and can be added to your diet for variety. Long the staple of diets in many Latin countries, beans can be prepared in countless numbers of delicious ethnic dishes. Although not my personal favorite, these inexpensive diet staples are a nearly perfect complex carbohydrate, though higher in calories than most vegetables. The fiber principle, however, says that you'll begin to feel full before you overindulge.

Fruits, the final group of carbohydrates, are a real godsend to those of us with a sweet tooth. You can eat any that you enjoy, with the exception of avocados and coconuts, which are higher in natural oils. Because fruit is high in fructose, a natural fruit sugar, it satisfies the need for a dessert item in the Star Dieter's menu. Fruits should be approached with some caution since they do add calories and those calories can add up. You don't want to overindulge. Compared to sugar, however, fruit is a far healthier choice.

As you incorporate these fiber-rich foods into your diet, you'll find that you'll be chewing more and eating less. You'll get the quick energy you need and feel full sooner and longer than with the simple carbohydrates.

Protein. Protein is found in meat, poultry, fish, dairy products, eggs, and beans. Experts tell us that proteins are the building blocks of life itself; only water is more plentiful in the human body. Protein is found in every living cell in our bodies, and it is responsible for the metabolic process of burning energy. Consuming the correct amount of protein provides the raw material for healthy teeth and bones, strong muscles, calm nerves, and beautiful skin. The body doesn't store protein, so a constant source of protein is very important. Nutritionists recommend that about 12–15 percent of total daily calories come from protein to maintain optimum health.

The problem, though, is that most Americans are consuming almost twice the recommended amount of protein a day. Since many of our protein foods also contain a high percentage of fat, the problem is compounded. Most animal foods are high in both calories and fat. A well-broiled 10-ounce porterhouse steak, for example, weighs in at 1,339 calories, 40 percent of which come from fat! Eating large pieces of meat, often recommended in high-protein diets, can make you think you're losing weight, but it's an illusion. What you are really experiencing is temporary water loss.

For years diet doctors have preached the wonders of protein. Many self-proclaimed nutritionists still advocate that a high-protein, low-carbohydrate diet is the best means to weight control. The idea is that since protein is responsible for the metabolic process, the more protein, the higher the metabolism. But it doesn't work this way. Instead of leading to permanent weight loss, extremely high-protein diets usually lead to the yo-yo cycle, where weight continually fluctuates. As with everything else, the key to protein consumption is moderation. Limit your intake to about 4–6 ounces of fish, poultry, or lean meats and choose from low-fat forms. Fifteen percent of the Star Diet calories is protein. That is more than enough to maintain health.

Vitamins and minerals. These nutrients are available both through diet and in supplement form. Although a wide range of vitamins and minerals are necessary for optimum health, I want to concentrate on several.

The supplement that is absolutely essential to Star Dieters who take advantage of the StarCaps is potassium. Because of the mild diuretic properties of the special garlic in StarCaps your body will be ridding itself of excess fluid on a regular basis. This can result in loss of potassium. Replenishing the potassium in your system is important to prevent muscle cramps and constipation.

It's one reason I suggest taking StarCaps with orange juice, a good source of potassium. Other excellent sources of potassium are spinach, bananas, melons, prunes, dates, raisins, and cranberry juice. For those taking StarCaps on a daily basis, a potassium supplement is also recommended.

Another important concern, especially for women, is iron and calcium. Just as protein builds muscles, calcium builds bones, and iron builds red blood cells. Medical studies show that women rarely consume as much as they need. Low calcium levels following menopause lead to osteoporosis, a potentially serious form of bone deterioration. Low iron . . . anemia. Both minerals are available in fresh foods: spinach, broccoli, and bok choy for iron; and dairy products, beans, and greens for calcium. Once again, it is also simple for women to ensure adequate calcium and iron intake through the use of a multivitamin supplement. Men, on the other hand, are in particular need of chromium, magnesium, potassium, selenium, and zinc.

Perhaps the nutrient with the highest current profile is beta carotene, a highly-touted antioxidant that joins with vitamins C and E to attack free radicals or mutant oxygen molecules in your blood and cells. Every day, these molecules are formed in the course of millions of routine chemical reactions within the body. These oxygen molecules are what make metal rust or a freshly sliced apple turn brown. These same molecules travel through the body doing damage to our cells. When the formation of these radicals gets out of hand, any number of health problems can result. They can lead to loss of flexibility in the blood vessels, weakening of the immune system, and even contribute to cancer. Beta carotene, vitamin C, and vitamin E gather up these free radicals so they can no longer do damage.

Beta carotene can be found in deep green and bright orange fruits and vegetables such as carrots, pumpkins, sweet potatoes, spinach, and cantaloupe. Vitamin C is found in orange juice, green peppers, strawberries, grapefruit juice, broccoli, and kiwi. The third member of the antioxidant team, vitamin E, can be found in almonds, wheat germ, peanuts, pecans, and vegetable oils.

Good daily supplements are available for all these vitamins and minerals. Some hints for supplement shopping: Read the label carefully to make sure of what you're getting. Potency varies widely. You don't really need more than 100 percent of the RDA for nutrients so don't waste your money on high-potency "megavitamins." Although they don't replace the nutrients found in food, supplements are an easy way to make certain you're meeting your body's needs.

BEST SOURCES OF ANTIOXIDANTS

Beta Carotene	Vitamin C	Vitamin E
Apricot	Apricot	Almonds
Broccoli	Broccoli	Brussels sprouts
Butternut squash	Cantaloupe	Hazelnuts
Cantaloupe	Grapefruit	Peanuts
Carrot	Kale	Spinach
Kale	Kiwi	Vegetable oils
Pumpkin	Orange	Wheat germ
Spinach	Pepper	
Sweet potato	Spinach	
Tomato	Strawberries	
	Turnip greens	

Fat. The F-word. We all hate to hear it, and we hate seeing it on ourselves even more. But it's a fact of life, so we'd better educate ourselves about it. Where fat is concerned, ignorance is definitely not bliss.

We've all heard about good fat and bad fat. Saturated fats are the "bad guys" of the fat kingdom. These are the fats found in animal products such as the fatty sections of beef, chicken, turkey, lamb, veal, and pork, as well as in dairy products like full-fat cheese and milk. Saturated fats are the ones you want to avoid as much as humanly possible.

Let me begin by telling you there is no such thing as truly good fat, a concept no doubt suggested by some very skinny person. Nevertheless, what people mean by "good fat" is unsaturated fat, the kind found primarily in various nuts, avocados, and vegetable oils. Unsaturated fats stay liquid at room temperature. "Good fat" can also refer to olive oil and canola oil, which have been shown to lower cholesterol, and to the omega-3 fatty acids in fish, which can lower the risk of heart attacks. A balanced diet should include a limited amount of these kinds of fats.

As usual, though, there's a catch. Even unsaturated fats can be ruined by a common process called hydrogenation. This is the process by which manufacturers add hydrogen to unsaturated fat to give it a longer shelf life. Unfortunately, that's not the only thing hydrogenation does. It also makes the previously unsaturated fat solid, in the process transforming it into saturated fat. Margarine is a perfect example of this process. Margarine labels are telling the truth when they say they were made from unsaturated fats. The key words here are "were" and "made from," which describes the vegetables oils in the margarine *before* processing. Misleading? You bet it is. Cross margarine off your "good list," or at the very least, limit the amount.

Does this mean that you should cut out fat entirely? Absolutely not. A limited amount of fat is essential to health. Our bodies need some fat to survive. Fat is one of the body's primary nutrients. It's an effective storehouse for vitamins A, D, E, and K, fat-soluble vitamins which require fatty molecules to be absorbed into the body. Fat slows down the aging process, prevents certain viral infections, and keeps the heart and blood vessels flexible. It insulates our bodies against cold and serves as an internal shock absorber, protecting our vital organs from bruising and rupturing. Fat is also essential to the production of certain hormones and provides a concentrated source of long-range energy.

The problem isn't that we eat fat, but that we eat so much of it. Average Americans get an astounding 35 percent of their calories from fat, enough to insulate an Eskimo through a long Arctic winter—or give a city dweller a heart attack. Even the American Heart Association's recommendation that you limit your fat intake to 30 percent is much too high. Believe me when I say that you'll never lose weight following that advice. To get and keep slim, you must limit your diet closer to 10 percent fat. This does not allow for cheese, butter, oily dressings, or fattening desserts. What it does allow for is the kind of fat you find in complex carbohydrates and certain low-fat proteins and dairy products. Keep in mind that for many people, cutting fat is the hardest part of a diet. But doing it will not only help you slim down; it will also eliminate one of the two primary causes of heart attacks (the other being smoking).

What does it mean to get your fat intake under control? You already know you must limit your daily fat intake to 10 percent of your diet, but now it's time to get down to the specifics of how to banish that fat dragon. You start by avoiding the following foods like the diet plague—they give "devil's food" a whole new meaning.

FOODS YOU CAN NEVER EAT OR DRINK (well, hardly ever)

Alcohol	Olives
Bacon	Pastrami
Carbonated drinks	Pastries
Full-fat cheese	Peanut butter
Chili (meat)	Pickles
High-fat chocolate	Pizza
Corned beef	Popcorn (buttered)
Cream (whipped or otherwise)	Pork
Frankfurters	Potato salad
Fried foods	Processed meats (bologna, salami)
French fries	Sausages
Gravies	Smoked fish or meat
Macaroni and cheese	Full-fat sour cream
Malteds and shakes	Sugar
Mayonnaise	Sundaes
Nuts	

All the foods on this list are loaded—often dripping—with calories. Including *any* of them in your diet can be almost "fatal." The only way to lose weight is to cut calories, and to cut them dramatically. Trying to lose weight without reducing your calorie intake is like trying to go down on an elevator while you're pressing the "open" button. You're not going to go anywhere with the door open. You have to close the door before you can go down. It's the same way with your weight.

Now don't think I don't know what you're thinking—no *chocolate* (or french fries, or whatever your particular downfall is). I understand, and I sympathize. Even as I write down this list, the truth is, every word sounds delicious. There isn't anything on the "limit" list I don't love, except perhaps for stinky bleu cheese, which wreaks havoc on your love life. I love a good salami on rye sandwich; in fact, I love all those fatty, salty, smoked meats. And as for fried foods, there's something about dipping something in batter and frying it in fat that makes us all salivate. Erasers would probably taste good cooked that way. Just smelling these foods makes me want to stampede to the nearest vendor for a double helping. But I know if I do, all my hard-earned weight loss will go down the drain. The best way I've found to cope with these cravings is the Elizabeth Taylor method: out of sight, out of mind. If you can't resist temptation, then learn to avoid it like the plague. Stay out of the corner deli. Run, don't walk, away from your favorite country-fried chicken outlet.

CHOCOLATE, THE DANGEROUS DELIGHT

For many people, especially women, the greatest tempter of all is chocolate. It's not for nothing that there are entire T-shirt lines dedicated to chocolate jokes. Some poor souls even claim they prefer chocolate to sex—a clear sign they need a new lover! Seductive as chocolate is, though, it becomes less tempting when we realize what we're really eating.

Cocoa itself isn't really all that bad. Mother Nature gave us the cocoa bean, from which we remove the fat and grind the bean into cocoa powder. So far, so good. The problem lies in what comes next. Because cocoa powder is bitter, we like to mix in sugar and fat to make it sweet, smooth, and succulent. By the time we're done, we've created a tasty concoction simply loaded down with fat and calories. Chocolate bars are so high in calories, in fact, that soldiers carry them as emergency rations in case of starvation.

For Star Dieters, though, starvation is the least of our problems. To complete the time bomb effect of a chocolate bar, it is simply loaded with caffeine, that addictive stimulant guaranteed to give you the jitters and sleepless nights. That's why caffeine is on the forbidden list for Star Dieters. We get high on life, not on artificial stimulants.

Another culprit that's probably sitting right on your dining table is the salt shaker. Humans do need a certain amount of sodium in their diets and the best source is salt, but Americans habitually pour much more salt on their food than anyone needs.

The average American consumes between 5,600 mg and 7,000 mg a day, up to twenty-three times the recommended daily intake of 500 mg. Sodium not only aggravates high blood pressure; it also causes excessive water retention. That's why high-salt foods like pickles and olives are on the "Don't" list. Take that salt shaker off the table and you'll see a dramatic drop in water retention that makes salt restriction well worth the trouble.

The final dishonorable mention goes to excessive alcoholic beverage intake. Technically, alcohol is a depressive drug, and alcoholic beverages a potentially nasty blend of calories and depressants. Too many rum and Cokes will leave you with hundreds of extra calories, an increased appetite, and an opening for a designated driver. Is it worth it? I don't think so.

Now that you're depressed from thinking about all the foods you *can't* eat, let me remind you of one of the principles of the Star Diet: It's not about what you can't eat, it's about what you *can* eat. The list of good foods you can eat freely is long.

THE NUTRITIONAL "STARS" OF THE STAR DIET

Artichokes	Grapes
Asparagus	Grapefruit
Bananas	Kiwi
Beans	Leeks
Broccoli	Lettuce
Brown rice	Mushrooms
Cabbage	Onions
Carrots	Oranges
Cauliflower	Peas

Pears	Strawberries
Rhubarb	String Beans
Rice	Tomatoes
Seafood	Turnips
Spinach	Watercress

Taken individually, the foods on this list each contribute to a balanced diet, so it's important to eat as many as possible. Citrus fruits provide antioxidants, with their powerful disease-fighting potential. Green foods are the lowest in calories and have the highest vitamin-mineral content of any food on the planet. Not a bad recommendation, especially when you consider that many of them are delicious.

All green vegetables are mildly laxative and, as such, prepare the body for peak functioning. One of the best is spinach, called the "broom of the stomach" in a French proverb. Spinach is not only high in iron; it is also a rich source of vitamins A and C.

Peas are another time-honored green vegetable. The simple peas goes farther back than recorded time. The oldest pea on record, unearthed near Thailand, was carbon dated at about 9,750 B.C.—For Star Dieters, though, a slightly younger pea is tastier, not to mention lower in calories. As peas grow and ripen, they gain starch and sugar, which means more calories. Baby peas are thus an ideal choice for dieters, since they are not only delicious but also lower in calories than their grown-up counterparts. Peas are a fair source of vitamins A and C, and a good source of niacin and iron.

Labeled by some as "man's best friend in the vegetable world," cabbage delivers a full plate of vitamin C with a pinch of vitamin A thrown in for good measure. Both broccoli and cauliflower are members of the cabbage family, along with Brussels sprouts and kohlrabi (admittedly, not favorites of mine). Mark Twain once called cauliflower "cabbage with a college education." Along with its green relative, broccoli, cauliflower gets high marks in both vitamin C and iron. Broccoli, the king of the vegetables, also provides vitamin A, riboflavin, and calcium.

The star of many a meal, the onion, was labeled by Robert Louis Stevenson as a "rose among roots," though technically it comes from the lily family. Along with leeks, the "poor man's asparagus," onions provide more flavor than nutrients, though they do have a fair amount of vitamin C. Rhubarb, most familiar in pies, is nevertheless a vegetable. Try the stalks, which are rich in vitamin A, but pass on the leaves— they're poisonous! One of my personal favorites, asparagus, is at its peak in April and May. A delicate vegetable, asparagus loses its vitamin content if it's even slightly overcooked, so don't leave it in the steamer too long. Properly prepared, this delicious vegetable provides a healthy portion of vitamin A as well as fair amounts of iron, vitamins B and C, and folic acid.

Then there's the lowly radish, always the bridesmaid but never the bride on a dinner plate. Best eaten raw, radishes provide tangy flavor but not much in the way of vitamins. Another flavor favorite, the mushroom, has been gracing plates for centuries. Found in everything from appetizers to desserts, the mushroom has been around for at least three hundred years, killing a few gourmets along the way. Russia's Alexander I, for example, died after eating a wild, toxic variety. Nowadays mushrooms are a lot safer, but not much more nutritious. Eat them for their subtle flavor, versatility, and for their extremely low calorie content.

Alexander I may have had a weakness for mushrooms, but King Henry VIII of England craved artichokes. Artichokes were once rumored to help produce male offspring, though I can't verify that personally. One thing I do know is that they are delicious. Once you get past the pointed edges, the nutty flavor is worth the effort.

New and Improved ...

In addition to choosing from the "Nutritional Stars" list, I've learned to transform some from the "Never" list into "not quite so bad foods." For example, I sometimes have a craving for a thick bacon, lettuce, and tomato sandwich on sourdough bread. While tomato and lettuce are on the good list, of course, bacon and bread are not. What to do? I substitute a soybean-based artificial bacon bit product for the fatty pork variety and use two big iceberg lettuce leaves in place of bread. It's delicious in itself, and it satisfies my BLT craving.

The last of my personal demons is the frankfurter. I love a good frankfurter, and in New York City, where they know good frankfurters, there's a stand on every corner. The catch is that, like sausage, frank-furters are over 80 percent fat! The other 20 percent, I can't account for. Clearly, I avoid these as much as possible, but I do have an emergency plan. I eat it without the bun. Apart from the calories I save by throwing away the bread, I've found that the mess alone forces me to quit before I'm halfway through. This emergency method works with any fatty, messy sandwich. Try it. You'll see what I mean.

All of which brings me to the bottom line. Nobody can live on veggies 24 hours a day. To think that you can never again eat a piece of chocolate or an ice cream sundae is so depressing that you'll want to quit. If you try to cut out your favorites completely, you'll fail. The key to sticking to the Star Diet is compromise. What that means in real life is that if you've been careful all week and lost a pound or two, reward yourself with a *taste* of something that you really love. I emphasize the word "taste." If chocolate is your downfall, eat one piece and throw the rest away—*immediately!* Keeping it for "later" is fatal. Get the tempting food out of sight and out of reach as quickly as you humanly can. Put it down the garbage disposal. Put it in the trash and then throw out the trash can. The idea was to give yourself a treat, not a binge. Have your treat, and then go right back on the program. This may take willpower, but the alternative—never touching the forbidden food again—takes even more. In the long run, it's also riskier. At some point you'll give in to the inevitable and eat the *whole* thing.

VICIOUS CYCLE

As a fellow dieter, I know the cycle. No matter how strong your willpower, no matter how great your dedication, no matter how careful your planning, sooner or later you will slip. You know this is true. Take a minute out for a reality check. The important thing is to accept your failures, and to move on. *Immediately* acknowledge what's happened, and *immediately* return to your game plan. Whatever you do, don't punish yourself. You don't deserve to be punished for being human. It will only make the problem worse. Accept that trial and error are all part of the process, and move on.

DON'T SLIP ON A BANANA

One last piece of advice on the subject of slipping. The most dangerous place for the Star Dieter isn't the kitchen; it's the supermarket. For dieters, the local market is a hotbed of temptation. More of us are undone in this one place than in any other. Beware! Know your enemy, and don't be caught unaware. Never enter this dangerous place unprepared: make sure you have your shopping list in hand before you put one foot inside. Prepare yourself by eating *before,* not after, your weekly journey.

A hungry shopper is a vulnerable one. Once inside the door, stick to your list. Do not give in to the temptation to browse. Don't embarrass yourself by snacking your way through the supermarket. We eat in dining rooms, *not* in stores. If you've fortified yourself with food before you arrive, this advice will be much easier to follow. Leave those chips labeled "lite" on the shelf where they belong. Skip the candy and ice cream aisles. Avert your eyes as you pass the deli and bakery sections. If you must linger, linger in the produce department.

When you get to the end of your list, get out of there as quickly as you can. You don't exactly need to run for your life, but you do need to get out the door before your willpower runs out. Luckily, the bounty provided by the Star Diet will still leave you plenty to choose from.

The list of fruits and vegetables, combined with an assortment of seafoods and other foods, allows you an enormous selection compared to other diet plans.

CHAPTER THREE

Labels—And I Don't Mean Armani

"FAT FREE doesn't mean you're home free."

With Charlton Heston at his Celebrity Shoot.

With Jason Priestly at Charlton's Celebrity Shoot.

All my life I've loved designer fashions. Knowing that the garment, pressed against my flesh is Chanel or Yves Saint Laurent or Valentino has always given me a thrill. I've been fortunate enough to know some of the top designers in the world, and over the years I've acquired a veritable treasure trove of designer fashions. Whether or not you have the good fortune to dine with the fashion world's elite, you can still take advantage of the most important labels in the world for the beauty-conscious—the Nutrition Facts label required by the Food and Drug Administration (FDA). Whether it is on the side or the back of the package, every box, can, and bag of food sold in America must bear this label. Labels from the top designers pale in comparison to this little number. Without it, we'd all be back in the diet Dark Ages.

The good news is that for the first time in history, it is possible for us to know the exact nutritional content of every morsel we consume. The bad news is that identifying the pertinent information on the label may not be as simple as it appears. Here is a "Nutrition Facts Label." Follow carefully as I guide you through the intricacies of the nutrition label maze. Don't worry—you'll soon get the hang of it.

★ **Serving Size.** This is our first stop. Always know the quantity of the portion that's being measured. In the past, this was tricky because manufacturers of high-calorie packaged foods would simply make the "serving size" incredibly small in an effort to make the product's calorie count look tiny. You thought you were eating 100

The Food Label at a Glance

The new food label will carry an up-to-date, easier-to-use nutrition information guide. The guide will serve as a key to help in planning a healthy diet.*

Serving sizes are now more consistent across product lines, stated in both household and metric measures, and reflect the amounts people actually eat.

The list of nutrients covers those most important to the health of today's consumers, most of whom need to worry about getting too much of certain items (fat, for example), rather than too few vitamins or minerals, as in the past.

The label of larger packages may tell the number of calories per gram of fat, carbohydrate, and protein.

Nutrition Facts

Serving Size ½ cup (114g)
Servings Per Container 4

Amount Per Serving

Calories 90   Calories from Fat 30

	% Daily Value*
Total Fat 3g	**5%**
Saturated Fat 0g	**0%**
Cholesterol 0mg	**0%**
Sodium 300mg	**13%**
Total Carbohydrate 13g	**4%**
Dietary Fiber 3g	**12%**
Sugars 3g	
Protein 3g	

Vitamin A 80%	•	Vitamin C 60%	
Calcium 4%	•	Iron 4%	

* Percent Daily Values are based on a 2,000 calorie diet. Your daily values may be higher or lower depending on your calorie needs:

	Calories:	2,000	2,500
Total Fat	Less than	65g	80g
Sat Fat	Less than	20g	25g
Cholesterol	Less than	300mg	300mg
Sodium	Less than	2,400mg	2,400mg
Total Carbohydrate		300g	375g
Dietary Fiber		25g	30g

Calories per gram:
Fat 9 · Carbohydrate 4 · Protein 4

New title signals that the label contains the newly required information.

Calories from fat are now shown on the label to help consumers meet dietary guidelines that recommend people get no more than 30 percent of their calories from fat each day.

% Daily Value shows how a food fits into the overall daily diet. It puts all nutrients on the same scale, so consumers trying to eat a more healthful diet will no longer have to remember what number is low for fat, saturated fat, cholesterol, and sodium, but can simply look for 5 or less on an individual food.

Daily Values are also something new. Some are maximums, as with fat (less than 65 grams); others are minimums, as with carbohydrate (300 grams or more). The daily values for a 2,000- and 2,500-calorie diet must be listed on the label of larger packages. Individuals should adjust the values to fit their own calorie intake.

calories of cake without ever knowing that you were *really* eating 100 calories *a bite!* It is good to know that the new serving sizes are more uniform from product to product and more closely represent the amount that people typically consume. It is also much easier to compare different brands of the same food for the best nutritional bargain. In the sample label, the serving size is "1 cup." If you eat two cupsful, then you must multiply all the nutrient amounts by 2. The weight of the serving is always listed to give you an idea of how big the standard serving is (in this case, 114 grams).

★ **Calories.** This line has two sections—total calories per serving and calories from fat per serving. These numbers are both very important to Star Dieters and, when coupled with the serving size and fat grams, represent the four most important figures on the entire label. Keep in mind that the calories listed refer to one serving. If you eat twice the amount that's listed, your calories will be double. For higher calorie foods, try to eat the amount listed on the label. It is easier to calculate your daily calorie total and you will not be going overboard.

The calories from fat are an important number for those wanting to keep track of the percent of calories from fat in their diet's. Fortunately, even the mathematically challenged can easily calculate the percent of fat in a given food. The formula is simple: Calories from fat divided by total calories multiplied by 100 equals percent of calories from fat. Keep in mind that your Star Diet should be close to 10–15 percent of calories from fat. If an individual food is a little higher in fat, just balance the rest of your meal with lower fat foods.

★ **Total Fat.** The fat grams in one serving are listed next. By definition, a low-fat food is one that has 3 grams of fat or fewer per serving. The more fat-free and low-fat foods you choose, the better. The Star Diet, which provides about 1,000 calories a day, has an average daily quota of about 16 grams of fat. Simply add up the fat grams for each food you eat to determine your actual daily fat gram intake.

★ **Cholesterol and Saturated Fat.** Unless you are on a medically restricted low-cholesterol diet, ignore these numbers. Since cholesterol is found only in animal products, the plant-rich Star Diet will not be a problem. You should know that the real culprit is saturated fat, which produces most of the cholesterol in the body, and the Star Diet is extremely low in saturated fat.

★ **Sodium.** Pay attention to this one. Although recent studies show most people can safely consume more sodium than was previously believed, anyone with high blood pressure consumes it at considerable risk. Even those of us who don't suffer from high blood pressure usually consume much more salt than we need, and since sodium greatly increases water retention, it's not something you want to abuse. The government recommends about 500–2,500 mg a day for all healthy people. I feel that 1,200 mg a day is more than enough to supply all the flavor we enjoy. Just remember to choose most often from foods that have 140 mg of sodium or less, and be careful with the salt shaker.

★ **Total Carbohydrate.** One truly useful number is the dietary fiber. The Star Diet is designed to be high in fiber, which can promote regularity and a feeling of satisfaction. For optimum health, Star Dieters should eat 100 percent of the government's suggested amount (25–35 grams) every day. While complex carbohydrates (starches) are the good guys, simple carbohydrates (sugar) can be trouble. Since the Nutrition Facts label includes both natural and added sugars, check the ingredient listing to see what type of sugar is added (if any).

★ **Protein.** The Star Diet calls for at least 35 grams of protein per day, about 15 percent of total calories. Ideally, this protein should be from low-fat sources such as fish, skinned poultry, and fat-free dairy products.

★ **Vitamins and Minerals.** Foods with at least 10 percent the RDA of a particular vitamin or mineral are considered a good source of that nutrient.

SHOPPERS QUICK TIPS

★ Your first stop should be the produce department. This is also where you should spend the most time and find the least amount of calories. Load your shopping cart with a wide variety of colorful fruits and vegetables. As a general rule, the brighter the color, the more nutritious the vegetable. You can't go wrong here.

★ Next, walk quickly past the meat department, stopping briefly for fresh fish, poultry, and the leanest meats. Generally, the center cut or any cut with the word "round" in it is the best meat choice. "Rib" is the worst (spare rib, prime rib, etc.) since these are the fattiest and highest in calories.

★ Proceed to the dairy aisle and choose only fat-free or low-fat milk, cheese, and yogurts. For the best nutritional buys, choose natural, not "processed," cheeses and yogurt with live, active culture.

★ Next, on to the breads and cereals. "Whole-grain" is the magic word here since these breads and cereals have a nutritional bonus—natural dietary fiber. Be careful to check the nutrition label on cereals since they can be loaded with sugar. Choose those with 5 grams of sugar or fewer per serving. Also, the healthiest cereals have 5 grams of fiber or more, and there should be fewer than 3g of fat in any cereal you choose.

★ The frozen food aisle runs the gamut from one nutritional extreme to the other. Plain frozen vegetables can be a godsend, since they are picked at their peak and flash-frozen to preserve nutrients. Sauces change the nutritional picture by adding loads of fat, calories, and salt. Check the label.

★ Walking down the beverage aisle, look for bottled water or sugar-free flavored water. An easy way to ensure that you get your 6–8 cups of water per day is to buy water in 2-quart (or-liter) bottles and drink one per day. Limit caffeine-containing, sugar-free cola beverages to an occasional can or glass. Choose fruit juices with little or no added sugar. The "lite" varieties are the best.

★ Choose all foods based on the Nutrition Facts label, looking for those with less than 3 gm fat, 40 calories or less, and 140 mg sodium for the best nutritional choices. I try to limit my time in the supermarket to no more than 15 minutes so I'm not tempted to buy anything that is not on my list.

★ If you don't have time to read labels as you're dashing into the supermarket on the way home from work, make it a point to identify *in advance* favorite brands and products to grab on those especially busy days.

★ If you are in a hurry and don't have time to be a nutrition detective, quickly reading the nutrition claim on the front of a package may signal a good choice for the Star Dieter. Terms such as "fat-free," "calorie-free," or even "low-fat" on the front mean that the product cannot exceed certain fat/calorie levels per serving and are usually a good Star Diet bargain. But make sure to confirm that the item actually does conform to the Star Diet guidelines once you get it home.

So get with it! The time you spend reading labels is well worth the benefits to your health and figure. After a while you'll become so well informed about your old favorites that you'll only need to read up on new favorites waiting to be enjoyed. The treasures you'll find along the way are well worth the search.

CHAPTER FOUR

Rub a Toad's Stomach and Other Diet Myths

"If excuses were dollars, we'd be millionaires."

I ran into Liza Minnelli at The Million Dollar Ball in Houston.

Having a laugh with Sharon Stone and Mel Tormé.

Roger Karnbad

Back in the days of my great-grandmother, dieting wasn't nearly as major an issue as it is today. Full-figured men and women were a sign of success. If you had money, you ate—and ate well. Only the poor exercised (call it physical labor) and ate large quantities of vegetables, which they could grow inexpensively themselves. A thin body was a sign of poverty, not of success.

Yet even then there were secret potions, elixirs, and myths which promised to help those who did want to shed a few strategic pounds. My personal favorite comes from a book of Pennsylvania Dutch home remedies:

> For the man, woman, or child with a thickened waist or thighs, get thee a toad, fresh from the pond, at the first dawn before a full moon. Prepare the toad by soaking a small towel in elderberry tea and placing the toad upon it. When the full moon be shining, grab thee the toad and carefully rub its stomach thrice in a clockwise fashion. After this be done, place the toad on the affected area and hold until the thickening releases.

No mention how long that might be.

While we may no longer use toads in the light of the full moon to exorcise unwanted fat, there are still a plethora of myths surrounding weight loss. Most of their origins have been lost, but the misinformation lingers on. Here are a few you may have acquired over the years.

You Can Spot-Reduce Through Exercise.

It's the number 1 myth in the diet industry. The cable channels and late-night television shows have been flooded with spot-reducing gimmicks for years, each with only six payments of $19.95. For years I have watched women exercise their thighs and hips, thinking they're going to slim down. I watched men do endless sit-ups in an effort to lose their bellies. Each shares a common misconception: that the fat attached to a certain part of their bodies belongs to that muscle group. That's not the way it works.

The only thing that belongs to the muscle group is the muscle. Your fat belongs to the *entire* body. You can do sit-ups until you're blue in the face, but you won't touch the layers of fat on top of the muscle. Your abdominal muscles may become hard as a rock, but no one will ever know. They will be hidden beneath the layers of fat. In order to reduce the amount of fat in a given spot, you must reduce the overall fat in your entire body. That's the only way it works. We all have stubborn fat areas that seemingly won't budge. And as luck would have it, they always seem to be in the very place we want to lose the fat first. Unfortunately, the only way to lose it is to persevere in your efforts to lose overall body fat. Stay on the Star Diet, continue your exercise routine, and eventually you will lose the fat, even from those problem spots.

Wearing Sweat Suits, Heat Belts, or Metallic Cover-ups Will Burn Fat Off Faster.

The comedy film *The Full Monty* shows a pudgy male would-be stripper wrapping his belly with cellophane wrap in a desperate attempt to melt away his flabby stomach. This misconception has been around since the days of the steam cabinet. "Melt fat away in minutes," the old advertisements told us. The image is that of fat disappearing from bacon in a hot frying pan. It seems plausible, especially if you're desperate, and modern infomercials continue to promote the concept. Advertisers offer rubberized belts which cinch your waist and thighs, increasing the body heat in those areas. A variation is heat belts which plug into the wall and generate an external heat source in your "problem areas." Even the ubiquitous sweat suit was originally designed to trap body heat in an effort to burn off the pounds. The idea was the more you sweat, the faster the fat burns. Their sister product, metallic sweat suits, are supposed to double the intensity.

It's an appealing concept, but it simply isn't true. Fat boils—and melts—at 360° Fahrenheit. Anything less than that, and you're not melting anything. So unless you're willing to set your sweat suit on fire, you're not accomplishing anything with your fat-melting gear. Those who have tried such products and insist they get results, consider this: the products don't melt fat; they relocate it temporarily. Remember the old bone corsets, that shifted women's waists up to their chests? It's pretty much the same concept. What these products do is to temporarily shift water weight from one area to another through the application of heat and pressure. When the area cools off, the flood gates open, and all the water comes rushing back. Take the confining apparatus off for long, and the fat will rush back to its original position.

If you want to wear a sweat suit to keep warm, fine. In fact, you should put one on for a short time after exercising, especially in cool weather, to prevent your muscles from cramping up. But beyond that, forget it. Using tight rubberized belts or leggings during exercise can actually be harmful. They constrict blood flow and muscle, preventing both from working optimally and slowing down the rate at which you burn fat in the process.

Starches Make You Fat.

This is a corollary to the "carbohydrates are evil" propaganda underlying all those no-carbohydrate diets. As the Star Diet makes clear, some starches such as baked potatoes and whole-grain breads are actually the good guys—in moderation. Complex carbohydrates are some of the fastest-burning foods you can eat, and provide your body with an almost immediate source of fuel. The only thing that burns quicker is sugar, a simple carbohydrate that burns in a flash. Unfortunately, sugar-fueled energy disappears as fast as it arrives—sort of an easy come, easy go principle.

Starches don't generate fat unless you eat too much or the wrong kind. What we put on top of them does even more harm. The problem isn't as much the baked potato as the mound of sour cream and butter we pile on it. So too with buttered bread and too much sauce. Starches are fine; just eat them in moderation with nonfat dressings or salsa. Follow this rule: Nothing processed and white—practically no white food at all while you're dieting; no refined white bread, white rice, ice cream, etc. All you will get is the goodness of the food and the energy it provides to burn the fat off your body.

Foods Labeled "Health Foods" Are Diet Foods.

This is exactly what the promoters of these products want you to think. They've made a fortune promoting these foods as keys to good health and weight control. And the fact is that they *look* healthy. It seems plausible that anything low in fat, high in fiber, and "good" for you will help you lose weight. Sadly, though, it's simply another heavily promoted illusion that has earned billions of dollars for its promoters. These foods are not only off-limits to the dieter; they're not even healthy.

Bran muffins top my personal list of bogus diet foods. While bran is, in fact, an excellent source of carbohydrates, calcium, phosphorus, and fiber, what happens to it when it is baked into giant muffins is appalling. What starts out as the outer layer of grains is processed with flour, fat, salt, honey (which is just as bad as sugar), and various flavorings until it's become the ultimate high-fat, low-nutrition food. If you want to eat bran, great, but check the label for fat and calorie content. If the muffin has less than 3g fat and around 100 calories, great. Better yet, get a bran cereal with a minimum of additives. Make jumbo, high-fat muffins a fond but distant memory.

While you're at it, donate the granola to a local food bank. Its reputation is as spurious as that of the mighty muffin. Why it's considered a health food has always been a mystery to me. Granola started out as a European breakfast food called muesli, developed by a nineteenth-century nutritionist named Dr. Bircher-Benner. *Muesli* is the German word for "mixture," and it is characterized by its blend of several ingredients. It originated as a blend of grains (primarily oats), dried fruit chunks, and chopped nuts rather like trail mix. Dr. Bircher-Benner added bran, wheat germ, sugar, and milk products to his list of ingredients. By the time muesli reached America, it had been renamed "granola." Although the specific ingredients vary by brand, the wheat germ and bran of the original muesli have disappeared and been replaced by fat, in the form of oil. The sugar content has also been increased. Granola cereal quickly became available as granola bars, making the food even more popular as a sort of portable breakfast. Unfortunately, this so-called "healthy breakfast" can be up to 78 percent fat, which accounts for its taste appeal. Even the new low-fat granola bars may not be a dietary bargain.

Check the Label!

Another advertiser's dream is the much-touted "healthy" candy, yogurt-covered raisins or nuts. They're usually sold in bins with other so-called health foods, or marketed in packages with trendy labels implying they are a healthy alternative to candy. Reaching for a package of yogurt-covered raisins instead of a bag of jelly beans makes you feel virtuous. A celebrated star famous for her tattoos loves to carry yogurt-covered raisins as her "healthy snack." Sadly, it's just another illusion. Not only are the snacks high in fat; they're not even coated with yogurt. Rather, the main ingredients in the white coating are sugar and hydrogenated palm kernel oil, a high-saturated fat that is absolutely off-limits to the dieter. While it's true that there is often (though not always) yogurt powder mixed in with the sugar, there isn't a single live bacteria culture in it to provide the health benefits ascribed to yogurt. You're better off just eating the raisins, or better yet, the grapes. They are high in water content, and they'll fill you up and satisfy your sweet tooth at the same time.

Juice-sweetened cookies, like yogurt-covered sweets, are another dessert trap for the unwary. The implication is that cookies sweetened with juice rather than sugar are somehow an improvement on the original. The catch is that whether you use juice or sugar as a sweetener, the calorie count remains the same. The culprit isn't the sugar; it's the fat. And just like ordinary cookies, their over priced counterparts may also be high in fat. Unless you reduce the fat, reducing the sugar is meaningless to the dieter. If you want juice, drink a glass. If you want dessert, grab a nonfat yogurt cone (but beware, the calorie count for most yogurt sold in yogurt specialty stores is underrated and more fattening than it may seem—if it sounds too good to be true, it probably is), and if you want to crunch, fill your cookie jar with pretzels.

Irritated as I am by phony claims of "healthy cookies," the so-called diet food that really sets me off is that enduring diet staple, cottage cheese. Somehow, somewhere, someone came up with the idea that an ice cream scoop of cottage cheese on a plate of fruit is dietetic. Worse yet, a scoop of cottage cheese with a hamburger patty is still sold in restaurants as a "diet plate." Who is kidding whom? Cottage cheese is 44 percent fat (never mind the hamburger patty). It triggers the body to release the same amount of cholesterol as any other fatty food. True, there are low-fat and even no-fat versions available at the supermarket, but it's nearly impossible to determine the fat content of the cottage cheese served at restaurants. If you want to eat fat-free cottage cheese at home, fine. But order it at restaurants at your own risk, knowing that what you're about to eat probably has as much fat as the rest of the menu.

The final item on my phony foods list is the all-popular sports drinks. Let the word "sports" be your first hint that they're not for the average dieter. These drinks were developed for high-intensity athletes in training who reach glucose utilization after 90 minutes or more of a peak performance workout. In other words, they replace blood sugar depleted by intense physical activity. If you read the labels on the bottles, you'll find that these drinks are mainly sugar and water. For all practical purposes, you might as well be drinking a bottle of cola without the caffeine. If you're a high-performance athlete, I very much doubt you need my weight-loss plan. For us common mortals, however, a bottle of water is a better choice. It will refresh and detox your system at the same time.

You Overeat Because You're Hungry.

Plausible but wrong. *By definition, you can only overeat if you're already full.* If you truly are hungry, if your stomach is growling and sending your brain signals that it needs food to drive the body's engine—then you are eating to supply needed fuel and nutrition. If you're eating for any other reason, you are overeating.

Unfortunately, this happens all too often. Research has shown that the primary cause of overeating is stress. We eat when we're worried, under pressure from deadlines, having family or romantic difficulties, or are in financial jeopardy. Compounding the difficulty is the fact that stress causes us to crave the worst kind of foods—those loaded with fat. When we're stressed, we reach for ice cream, cream-filled chocolates, or popcorn dripping with butter. Fortunately, there are other ways to survive cravings than by stuffing yourself with fattening foods. Sometimes just waiting is enough; a craving may pass as quickly as it came. If waiting it out doesn't work for you, try substituting a stress-relieving activity.

The More You Exercise, the Better.

Again, this is logical, and to some extent, it's also true. Unless you become addicted to exercise (as some do), you will lose weight faster if you exercise with all the vigor of Sly Stallone or Cher. Working out at a gym three hours a day will burn fat faster than walking around the block three times a week. The problem is that most of us aren't going to keep up that pace, at least not for long. A few weeks of intense workouts is about as much as most of us can stand. Human nature suggests that we won't keep it up.

The credo is this: The best exercise for you is the one you'll actually do. It is far better to choose a moderate exercise program that you enjoy (or at least don't hate) and stick to it than to choose a back-breaking routine you'll abandon. Any exercise is better than none at all. According to the American College of Sports Medicine, 60 percent of all Americans do no exercise at all. For these people to jump directly into a high-impact, high-intensity workout is not only foolish but dangerous. If you're part of that 60 percent, the key is to start slow and to stick with it. Persistence, not intensity, is the key. As you feel better and begin to lose weight, your ego will encourage you to keep it up. Your ego will remind you that you shouldn't skip exercising without a good reason, and it will also praise you when you follow through on your promises to yourself. After a while the cycle will become self-perpetuating, and you won't want to give up the healthier, more toned body your exercising has earned you.

The Average Person Burns Approximately 2,500 Calories a Day.

Oh, that this were true. If it were, we could all have fries for lunch every day and abandon exercise forever.

For years this piece of fallacious data was widely preached by physicians and nutritionists everywhere. The belief was that since the average person burns approximately 2,500 calories per day, eating less than that amount would result in weight loss. Diets were accordingly planned so that the dieter would eat approximately 2,000 calories or so in the course of a day. "Crash diets" might call for 1,200 calories, but that level was considered extreme.

The problem was that rather than constituting a crash diet, 1,500 calories a day is actually the maximum number of calories most of us can eat and lose any weight at all. For many people, especially women, under 1,000 calories is a more realistic figure. It turns out that earlier beliefs about metabolic rate and caloric requirements were wrong. Recent research has shown that the resting metabolic rate is actually much lower than previously believed. According to a study in the American Physiological Society's *Journal of Applied Physiology,* the average woman's resting metabolism burns 1,340 calories a day, and a man's approximately 1,400. Those numbers can be raised by physical activity; the more active you are, the more those numbers will elevate during the course of the day. For people who lead a sedentary lifestyle, however, their metabolism never rises much above the resting rate. That means that if you don't do physical labor for a living, you probably don't burn much more than 1,400 calories on an average day. Obviously, counting calories will not be enough for you to maintain a goal weight. You will have to raise your metabolic rate through exercise.

I'm Overweight Because I Have a Slow Metabolism.

What a grand and glorious rationalization this is. I've heard it all my life. Implicit in this statement is not only that being overweight isn't our fault, but also that there's nothing we can do to change it. It's so comforting to believe that our weight problem can be explained away by big bones or faulty genes. But the trouble is that, with rare exceptions, being overweight has little to do with either our genes or our bones.

It is true that some people's natural metabolism works much faster than others. Everybody has a skinny friend who can eat anything she wants and never put on weight. But if you're not one of those people, guess what? You're not the exception; you're the rule. If you are one of those people who put on 10 pounds just from looking at a plate of cookies, you fall into the category most of us do. One family holiday or night on the town, and stepping on the scale is like a slap in the face. Every morsel you ate the day before shows up in the numbers next to your bare toes. I know. I have that scale, too. As far as I'm concerned, all scales are 10 pounds overweight—I couldn't possibly weigh that much!

But just because you don't have one of those super metabolisms doesn't mean that you're hopelessly doomed to being overweight all your life. On the contrary, you're still the one in control of your own weight, or more specifically, your own metabolism. Our metabolic rates aren't carved in stone. They can be changed. The trick to losing weight, and keeping it from coming back, is speeding up the metabolic rate at which you burn food. To do that, you will need to do three things.

The first step is to eat the right foods. As the Star Diet makes clear, the right foods are those complex carbohydrates and protein foods that are low in fat. Your body has to work to convert complex carbohydrates to fat, and it burns calories in doing so. Fat, on the other hand, is the body's answer to a lazy metabolism. It's just so easy, so painless for your body to metabolize fat. And our bodies are very, very good at storing it.

The human body was programmed centuries ago to protect itself against starvation. Like a camel preparing for a journey across the desert, our bodies are constantly tucking away fat in case of emergency. The practical difficulty for most of us, however, is that the emergency never arrives. We have too much food, not too little. The federal government tells us that up to 30 percent of our diet should be fat. Not even close. A more realistic figure is 10 percent for the Star Dieter.

The second step in speeding up your metabolism is to get your body moving. If you want to burn fuel, you have to move. Your car doesn't burn much gasoline while it's sitting in the garage. Neither will you while you're sitting in your living room. The ideal form of exercise for increasing the metabolism is aerobics combined with calisthenics.

Whatever form of exercise you choose, however, you must do it regularly to see results. Just half an hour a day can make a world of difference. Make exercise as much a part of your schedule as brushing your teeth.

CHAPTER FIVE

The Star Diet: Seven Days to a New and Better You

"The five word diet formula: Eat Less and Exercise More."

With Hillary Clinton and Beverly Johnson during the 1997 Inaugural festivities.

Backstage with Tony Bennett.

The Star Diet Seven-Day Meal Planner is designed to give you a framework that will jump-start your weight loss program. It includes seven days of breakfasts, lunches and dinners with a variety of foods that are low in calories, low in fat, and taste great.

★ **Pay special attention to the amounts of each food.** Portion control is the key to controlling calories and weight. The daily calorie totals are under 1,000, and approximately 10 percent of total calories are from fat. This is deliberately lower than you are probably used to so you can begin to experience desired weight loss immediately.

★ **Customize to your particular food preferences.** For example, you can substitute any comparable vegetable that you prefer for the vegetable in the meal plan or substitute any fish or poultry selection for those listed. This will help you to adhere to the plan long term. You can even enjoy dining out using the same principles. I also recommend taking a multi-vitamin every day.

★ **Star Dieter's Diary.** I have created a Diet Diary that helps you to keep track of your daily food intake and weight loss success. My clients have had the greatest weight loss results when they keep their food record religiously. (See Appendix II)

★ **Exercise.** It is important to increase your activity level to burn excess calories and produce a sense of well-being. Any activity is good, but following the advice in chapter 9 will produce the best results.

★ **Maintenance.** Once you have achieved your desired weight loss, then maintenance is the next step. You will have developed new eating and exercise habits that you will carry with you for the rest of your life. During maintenance, you should follow the basic Star Diet meal plan, exercise, and occasionally have a special treat. You will find that by incorporating healthy planning into your life, you will develop the good habits that free you from the ongoing diet war.

STAR DIET TIPS

★ Start your diet on a Monday. Weigh yourself and plan to keep a diary.

★ Weigh yourself every third day in the morning. *Never* at night.

★ Every morning, get up and make sure you say to yourself, "I am going to eat right today." Take it one day at a time.

★ Put a "before" picture of yourself on your refrigerator.

★ Set diet goals. Decide how much weight you want to lose but be realistic. If you have 50 pounds to lose, set goals in 1-pound increments. You cannot lose 50 pounds in a week, as much as we all wish. Take a dress or a pair of slacks that you are not able to get into and see how long it takes for you to zip that zipper.

★ Don't keep anything fattening in the house to eat. Get rid of foods that are overly tempting.

★ Plan ahead. Decide what you're going to eat for the day and where you're going to eat it. Avoid problems.

★ Balance your meals. Fewer calories is not the only goal; it is also important to have calories that are good for you. Make sure that what you eat also keeps you healthy.

★ Drink lots of water throughout the day. Water will help fill you up, keep your mouth busy and help clean out your system.

★ Take small bites and serve your food on small plates. The food will seem like more and fill you up faster.

★ Take one bite at a time and chew slowly and thoroughly. It will help you eat less.

★ Don't eat off other people's plates. It's just as fattening even if you didn't order it.

★ When shopping, only buy foods that you need for your diet. Never go shopping when you are hungry and always shop with a list. It is a proven fact that the less food you buy, the less you'll be tempted to overeat.

★ Don't cook more food than you need.

★ To help kill the desire for food between meals, brush your teeth and rinse your mouth with mouthwash to curb the urge to splurge.

★ Don't panic if you go off your diet. Start again the next day— or the next hour.

★ Diet with someone. Help each other along.

★ Make sure you go out to dinner with people who are either on a diet or are health conscious. In other words, don't eat with someone who orders three entrées and five desserts then takes home two sandwiches.

★ Find a hobby that will keep your hands busy and away from food.

★ Figure out what times, other than mealtimes, you get hungry and keep a supply of StarSuckers™ or NikkiBars™ on hand to satisfy your cravings.

★ Bring your lunch to work with you. That way you will be able to decide, before you are hungry, what you will eat that day.

★ The trick to losing weight is *not* to starve yourself. Have an apple, celery, or any other fruit or vegetable.

★ Try not to eat late. If you do, don't go to sleep until 2 hours later.

★ If all else fails, eat your meals naked in front of a mirror!

★ Think thin.

★ If you desperately want something sweet and you have no StarSuckers around, chew on a small slice of lemon or a piece of fruit.

★ Never take food home from a restaurant. No doggie bags!

★ You can hire anyone to wash your car, paint your house or cut your hair, but remember, no one can lose weight for you.

★ Remember: Nobody's perfect. If you slip up, start over. Don't give up.

DAY ONE

Breakfast		*Calories*
6 oz orange juice or ½ grapefruit		75
1 Rye Krisp		20
	Total	95

Lunch

Nikki's Niçoise Salad*		240
4 tbsp Nikki's All-Purpose Dressing*		10
1 small breadstick		15
1 cup Fabulous Fresh Fruit Salad*		50
	Total	315

Dinner

4 oz Nikki's Famous Broiled Chicken*		180
2 cups broccoli or green beans, steamed with lemon		50
2 cups tossed salad: lettuce, celery, mushrooms, onion, and tomato		30
2 tbsp Nikki's All-Purpose Dressing*		5
1 melba toast		10
Dessert: 1 cup fresh whole strawberries		50
	Total	325

TOTAL CALORIES: 735

*Recipe follows.

DAY TWO

Breakfast

	Calories
6 oz orange juice or grapefruit	75
1 piece whole wheat toast	60
2 tsp apple butter	20
½ cup skim milk or ½ cup fat-free sugar-free yogurt	40
Total	195

Lunch

Nikki's Bull's Eye*	170
½ cup fresh berries (raspberries, blueberries, etc.)	40
1 Rye Krisp	20
Total	230

Dinner

5 oz broiled scallops	100
½ cup steamed carrots and six asparagus spears	55
2 cups tossed salad: lettuce, celery, mushrooms, onion, and tomato	30
2 tbsp Nikki's All-Purpose Dressing*	5
Dessert: 1 cup fresh pineapple cubes	75
1 fat-free whole-grain cracker	15
Total	280

TOTAL CALORIES: 705

*Recipe follows.

DAY THREE

Breakfast		*Calories*
6 oz orange juice or ½ grapefruit		75
I cup whole-wheat cereal flakes		110
½ cup skim milk		40
	Total	225

Lunch

4 oz turkey breast, sliced in strips		140
served on a bed of lettuce with sliced tomatoes		15
topped with 2 tbsp Nikki's All-Purpose Dressing		5
I cup broccoli, steamed with lemon		25
I slice whole-wheat bread with mustard, if desired		70
Nikki's Slim Smoothie*		120
	Total	375

Dinner

4 oz cup cooked angel hair pasta topped with Primavera Pasta Sauce**		285
I cup fresh melon cubes		50
	Total	325

TOTAL CALORIES: 925

*for something fun, try turning your turkey salad into a turkey sandwich, using lettuce leaves as "a wrap."

**Recipe follows.

DAY FOUR

Breakfast   *Calories*

6 oz orange juice or ½ grapefruit		75
I cup oatmeal made with skim milk and sugar substitute, if desired		185
	Total	260

Lunch

Tomato Delight*		85
I pita pocket		105
I cup fresh grapes		60
	Total	250

Dinner

4 oz veal paillard (veal cutlet pounded thin), grilled/broiled with lemon		205
I cup steamed green beans		40
½ small baked potato		75
topped with 2 tbsp Mama Mia's Authentic Mexican Salsa*		5
⅓ cup Nikki's Cool as a Cucumber Salad*		35
I cup Fabulous Fruit Salad*		80
	Total	440

TOTAL CALORIES: **950**

*Recipe follows.

DAY FIVE

Breakfast		*Calories*
6 oz orange juice or ½ grapefruit		75
I cup strawberries topped with I tbsp fat-free yogurt		45
½ small bagel, scooped out		65
topped with I tbsp fat-free cream cheese		20
	Total	205

Lunch		
Shrimp Salad Supreme*		130
I small whole-grain dinner roll		70
I cup Fabulous Fruit Salad*		80
	Total	280

Dinner		
5 oz white fish broiled with lemon		130
I cup mixed steamed vegetables: broccoli, onion, carrots, mushrooms		50
2 cups tossed salad: tomatoes, radishes, cucumber, and chopped lettuce		30
2 tbsp Nikki's All-Purpose Dressing*		5
2 small breadsticks		30
	Total	245

TOTAL CALORIES:　730

*Recipe follows.

DAY SIX

Breakfast   *Calories*

6 oz orange juice or ½ grapefruit		75
I small fat-free oat bran muffin		115
½ cup skim milk		40
	Total	230

Lunch

Tomato Suprise*		100
served over 3 oz drained water packed tuna		75
2 small breadsticks or 2 Rye Krisp		30
	Total	205

Dinner

4 oz roasted turkey breast		140
I artichoke, steamed		25
2 cups tossed salad: mixed greens, cucumber, and mushrooms		30
2 tbsp Nikki's All-Purpose Dressing*		5
Nikki's Diet Candy Apple*		130
	Total	330

TOTAL CALORIES: 765

*Recipe follows.

DAY SEVEN

Breakfast

6 oz orange juice or ½ grapefruit		75
1 cup Cream of Wheat made with skim milk		210
	Total	285

Lunch

Nikki's Chop Suey*		125
½ cup whole kernel corn		70
½ cantaloupe		50
	Total	245

Dinner

4 oz filet of sole grilled with lemon		130
½ cup rice, preferably brown		85
1 cup steamed Brussels sprouts		60
1 cup strawberries or melon cubes		50
	Total	325

TOTAL CALORIES: 855

*Recipe follows.

THE RECIPES

Nikki's Niçoise Salad

A major hit on the French Riviera, this low-calorie version of the continental classic is satisfying and nutritious!

3   oz tuna fish, packed in water
1   cup chopped onion
4   radishes
½   cucumber, peeled and seeded
½   cup green beans
½   bell pepper
1   medium tomato
1   medium head romaine lettuce (about 2 cups)

Rinse and drain tuna. Place it in a large bowl. Chop remaining ingredients except lettuce and tomato. Mix with tuna until thoroughly blended.

Quarter tomato and break lettuce head into leaves. Arrange on a plate. Arrange tuna mixture on lettuce and enjoy!

Serves 1
Per serving: calories: 240   fat: 1 g

Nikki's All-Purpose Dressing

This is the best low-calorie dressing you'll ever taste.
It will add a burst of flavor to salads, seafood,
and vegetables of all kinds.

8	tbsp balsamic vinegar
3	tbsp water
2	packet sugar substitute
2	tbsp Dijon mustard

Place all ingredients in a small cup and mix well.

Yield: ½ cup
Per serving: calories: 5 per 2 tbsp fat: 0

Primavera Pasta Sauce

2	medium tomatoes, peeled and diced
1	cup sliced zucchini
½	cup of sliced mushrooms
2	tbsp chopped onions
2	tbsp fresh basil, chopped
3	tbsp of water

Combine ingredients in saucepan and heat, stirring often. Serve over any kind of pasta.

Yield: 1 cup
Per serving: calories: 85 fat: 0

Nikki's Famous Broiled Chicken

4 chicken breasts, with skin

MARINADE

2 cups orange juice
1 sprig fresh dill, chopped
1 tbsp cinnamon
4 tbsp low-sodium soy sauce
1 tsp pepper

In a medium-size bowl, combine marinade ingredients and mix well.
Clean chicken, scrape skin, and rinse under hot water.
Place in ovenproof dish.
Add marinade and leave for 2 hours, turning once.
Preheat oven to 300°. Cover dish with foil and bake chicken for 40 minutes.
Set oven to broil. Remove foil and broil chicken, basting and turning until brown on both sides, about 15–20 minutes. Test for doneness.
Remove skin before serving. Serves 4.

Optional: Place 1 cup of Fabulous Fruit Salad over chicken breasts 4 minutes before it is finished cooking.

Per serving: calories: 180 fat: 3 g

Nikki's Bull's Eye

*This high-energy and colorful recipe originated in
the kitchen of New York's 21 Club.*

½   **cup zucchini**
½   **cup carrots**
¼   **cup cauliflower**
½   **cup string beans**
½   **onion**
¼   **cup broccoli**
½   **mushrooms**
1   **egg**

Cut up all the vegetables into bite-size pieces and steam until tender.

Drop a fresh egg into barely simmering water until poached (about 4 minutes).

Place steamed vegetables on a plate and top with poached egg.

Hint: Poached eggs may be prepared in advance and kept for two to three days in the refrigerator. After poaching, dip immediately into iced water to stop cooking process and chill. Place uncovered in refrigerator until ready to use. Steam with vegetables.

Per serving: calories: 170   fat: 5 g

Nikki's Slim Smoothie

*If you like milk shakes, you'll love this
great dessert drink.*

Combine ½ cup of any of the following two fruits: raspberries, straw-berries, blueberries, pineapple, peaches, or bananas. Put in blender with 2 large tbsp of plain yogurt and ½ cup skim milk, and blend till foamy.

Makes 1 shake
Per serving: calories: 120   fat: 1 g

Fabulous Fruit Salad

Cut and mix together the following fresh fruits: berries, kiwi, pineap-ple, melons, and grapes. Add sugar substitute, as desired. Scoop out portion as per Star Diet.

Per serving: calories: 50   fat: 0

Tomato Delight

Despite its simplicity, this recipe never fails to bring compliments from my Star Diet Family.

1   **medium firm tomato**
½   **green pepper**
1   **stalk celery**
2   **radishes**
¼   **onion**
¼   **cucumber, peeled**
Nikki's All-Purpose Dressing (recipe above)

Scoop out center of tomato to form a bowl. Chop remaining vegetables and place in bowl. Top vegetables with Nikki's All-Purpose Dressing, mixing well. Place vegetables into tomato, allowing overflow to decorate plate. Refrigerate for 1 hour before enjoying.

Per serving: calories: 65 to 75 with dressing   fat: 0 g

Mama Mia's Authentic Mexican Salsa

From Chef Philip Haughey, SAM'S Classic Grille &
Superior Catering, McKeesport, Pennsylvania.

1   **cup fresh tomatoes, chopped fine**
1   **tbsp cilantro or oregano**
1   **tsp salt**
½   **tsp pepper**
pinch of sugar (use substitute)
2   **tbsp Tabasco juice**
½   **tsp garlic, minced**
2   **tbsp each chopped onions and green onions**

Combine all ingredients and mix well. Use as a dip, with fish or
scrambled eggs, or as a topping for Mexican dishes.

Makes about 1½ cups. Can be doubled.
Per serving: calories: 8 per 2 tbsp   fat: 0

Nikki's Cool as a Cucumber Salad

Easy to make, this salad lasts for at least a week and tastes great.

1	**cup white vinegar**
½	**cup water**
2	**packets sugar substitute**
2	**medium cucumbers, peeled and sliced**
1	**onion, chopped**

fresh chopped dill
season to taste with pepper

Combine white vinegar, water, and sugar substitute. Add remaining ingredients. Put in refrigerator to marinate. For a change of pace, add 1 cup of lettuce.

Per serving: calories: 115 fat: 0 g

Shrimp Salad Supreme

Of all my low-calorie meals, this is my personal favorite. Nothing about this salad says "diet".

4   **large shrimp, cooked**
½   **cup celery, chopped**
½   **medium apple, cored and chopped**
1   **tsp low-calorie mayonnaise**
1   **tsp Dijon mustard**
2   **cups lettuce**

Mix all ingredients except lettuce. Arrange lettuce on a plate and top with salad mixture. For variation, add ½ cup steamed green beans.

Per serving: calories: 130   fat: 1 g

Tomato Surprise

The real surprise is the great taste; goes with fish, veal, and chicken.

- 4 **tomatoes**
- 1 **sprig of dill, chopped**
- ½ **cup chopped onions**
- ½ **cup chopped celery**
- 1 **tsp parsley**
- 4 **tbsp Nikki's All-Purpose Dressing**

Put tomatoes in boiling water for about 2 minutes until skins break, then peel away skins. Cut into quarters, Add dill, parsley, celery, and onion. Add dressing, cover, and put in refrigerator for 2 hours to marinate.

Per serving: calories: 75 fat: 0 g

Nikki's Chop Suey

*We've taken some liberties with the Chinese favorite
and created our own bit of healthy magic.*

½   **cup low-fat cottage cheese**
¼   **cup chopped celery**
¼   **cup chopped green pepper**
¼   **cup chopped tomato**
¼   **cup chopped cucumber**
2   **radishes, chopped**
¼   **onion, chopped**
  salt and pepper to taste

Combine all ingredients in a large bowl and mix well. Place on plate in three scoops surrounded by parsley.

Per serving: calories: 125   fat: 1 g

Nikki's Diet Candy Apple

A special treat to satisfy your sweet tooth.

3   **tbsp diet cola or diet root beer**
1   **packet sugar substitute**
1   **large apple, cored**

Preheat oven to 450°. Mix soda and sugar substitute in small cup. Place apple in baking dish and pour sweetening mixture over top. Bake about 15 minutes or until apple is glazed and tender.

    Also works great with one half grapefruit.

Makes 1 apple
Per serving: calories: 130   fat: 0 g

SOUPS ON!

One of the best ways to curb hunger is to have good homemade soup in the house. It has been shown that chicken soup relieves the symptoms of a cold, sore throats, and the flu. In the fall and winter, I always keep a pot of soup on the stove. In fact, my friends often take advantage of my own little soup kitchen by sending over pots or glass containers and saying "fill them up."

Tony Curtis loves all my soups, but his favorite is my cold beet borscht. Alan Carr and Joan Collins rave about my chicken soup, and I am always happy that they ask for more.

Soup is really easy to make and it's the perfect way to fool your stomach, since it's dietetic, very filling, and good for you. Make the soup and drink it in a small cup, like an espresso cup. Have it before lunch or dinner, at a party, or as a meal replacement.

Spectacular Spinach and Leek Soup

2   **lbs fresh spinach**
2   **large leeks cut in pieces, leaving on most of the tops**
1   **bunch dill, or 1 tbsp dried dill**
2   **medium sprigs parsley, or ¼ cup dried parsley**
2   **medium onions, chopped coarsely**
dash cayenne pepper
salt and pepper
6   **cups water**

Wash the spinach well and drain. Spinach is very sandy, so make sure you get it clean. Chop the spinach, leeks, dill, and parsley by hand or in a food processor. Add remaining ingredients. Bring to a boil, then reduce to simmer and cook for 10 minutes. Serve chilled or hot.

Per serving: calories: 35 per cup   fat: 0 g

Sweet and Sour Cabbage Soup

12	cups water
5	small heads white cabbage
6	cups yellow onions
5	(1-lb) cans whole peeled tomatoes
6–8	lemons
1	bunch parsley, tied
1	bunch dill, tied
1	tbsp pepper
1	tbsp Dijon mustard
¼	cup sour salt to taste, found in specialty stores (may add more to taste)
3	tbsp sugar substitute (may add more to taste)
3	tbsp brown sugar
6	beef bouillon cubes
6–7	bay leaves
1	tbsp baking soda (eliminates gassiness)

Pour the water into a large pot. Cut the cabbage in quarters. Add the onions cut in quarters, and the tomatoes. Squeeze lemons. If you don't have fresh lemons, use lemon concentrate. When the cabbage has cooked down, add the rest of the ingredients. Cover soup and cook till tender, about 1½ hours. Remove the bunch of parsley before serving.

The cabbage soup lasts at least 7 days and freezes great.

Per serving: Calories: 50 calories per cup   fat: 0 g

Nikki's Diet Vegetable Soup

6   **carrots, cut in pieces**
6   **celery stalks, cut in pieces**
4   **cups coarsely chopped onions**
5   **tomatoes, skinned and chopped**
2   **parsnips, cut in quarters**
2   **medium turnips, cut in quarters**
2   **leeks, cut lengthwise**
1   **bunch parsley, tied together**
1   **bunch fresh dill, chopped, or 1 tbsp dried dill**
12   **cups water**
2   **tsp pepper**
6   **bay leaves**
1   **tbsp Dijon mustard**

Clean and peel vegetables. In a large pot, combine all ingredients. Cook on medium flame for 1½ hours. The first 45 minutes, cook with the lid off so the soup will cook down. Cover for the remaining 45 minutes, making sure the soup doesn't boil over.

When vegetables are tender, the soup is ready. This soup will last all week. Season to taste (may also add crushed red pepper to taste).

Per serving: calories: 70 calories per cup   fat: 0 g

Marvelous Beet Borscht

All your guests will ooooh and aaaah. They will think
that you have worked for days to make this soup.
Don't tell them how easy it really is.

1   **bunch green onions**
3   **cucumbers, cleaned and peeled**
2   **quarts of Manischewitz Beet Borscht**
1   **bunch of dill, or 1 tbsp dried dill**
1   **tbsp beef bouillon, or 3 bouillon cubes**
3   **tbsp fat-free sour cream**

Cut green onions and cucumber into pieces. Drain liquid from the
borscht soup into the blender. Leave the beets in the bottom of the
jar.

Add ¾ of the green onions, cucumber, and dill to the liquid. Add
the beef bouillon and a little sour cream and blend. The soup should
be light pink in color. Pour blended soup into a bowl and add in the
beets. Cover the soup and refrigerate for 2 hours.

To serve, add remaining cucumber, green onions, and dill as a
garnish.

Per serving: calories: 30 per cup   fat: 0 g

Gazpacho Soup

8–10	large tomatoes
3	cucumbers
2	green bell peppers
1	medium yellow onion
3½	tbsp vinegar
1½	tsp freshly ground black pepper
dash of Tabasco sauce	
1	pinch of cumin seeds
¼	cup chopped parsley or cilantro
1	tpsp light olive oil
1	tpsp chopped dill

Boil water and drop in tomatoes for 2 minutes until their skin pops. Take the skin off. Using a blender or food processor, blend tomatoes, and all other ingredients until pureéd. Serve chilled with diced tomatoes, cucumber, and green peppers as a garnish.

Per serving: calories: 50 per cup   fat: 0 g

ALL ABOUT ARTICHOKES

Artichokes are one of my favorite foods. If you're not familiar with artichokes, here are a few facts. Artichokes are an ideal food for a low-fat diet. The artichokes is a low-calorie, low-sodium, high-fiber, vegetable that is free of saturated fat and cholesterol. Additionally, it is an excellent source of vitamin C, magnesium, folate and provide small amounts of vitamin A and potassium. One artichoke contains only about 25 calories!

Selecting artichokes.   Choose artichokes that are heavy for their size; compact and firm in the winter and spring; a little flared and conical in the summer and fall.

Storing artichokes. Fresh artichokes will last about a week in your refrigerator, if you sprinkle them with water and put them in a plastic or large Ziploc bag.

Preparing artichokes. Artichokes can be boiled or steamed, and are very easy to prepare. First, rinse them in cold water and cut the stem off at the base. Cut off the points of the artichoke with scissors. To boil, simply bring enough water to cover the top of the artichoke to a rolling boil. Add a little salt and lemon juice. Place the artichoke in the boiling water, reduce heat, cover, and cook for 25 to 40 minutes (depending on size). To steam, use about three inches of water, and stand the artichoke up in the pan on a rack above the water. Cover, and boil for the same amount of time. When a petal near the center can be pulled out easily, it's done. Artichokes can also be cooked in a microwave. For a typical 700 watt microwave, a medium artichoke will take about 6 or 7 minutes to cook if set upside down in a ¼ cup of water, in a microwave-safe bowl. Let the artichoke stand covered for about 5 minutes when you take it out. Serve hot or cold.

Here are two of my favorite artichoke recipes:

Warm Artichoke and Scallop Salad

2   large California artichokes, prepared and cooked
    as directed for whole artichokes
12 oz bay scallops
½   cup lime juice
2   tbsp each chopped cilantro stems and leaves
2   tsp sugar
1   tsp cornstarch
3   drops hot pepper sauce
½   cup grated Swiss cheese

Cut artichokes in half lengthwise and cut off points with scissors. Remove center petals and fuzzy centers. Place scallops, lime juice, and cilantro stems in a microwave-safe container; marinate 10 minutes. Cover with waxed paper; microwave at medium (50%) power for 5 minutes. Remove scallops from marinade. Strain marinade into microwave-safe container; stir in cilantro leaves, sugar, cornstarch, and hot pepper sauce. Microwave at full power for 2 minutes. Arrange scallops on each artichoke half; drizzle with heated mixture. Garnish with cheese. Microwave at medium power 2 minutes or until thoroughly heated.

Serves 4
Per serving: calories: 155   fat: 4 g

Artichokes with Smoked Salmon Pasta Salad

4   medium-size California artichokes, cooked
8   oz orzo pasta
½   cup plain yogurt
½   cup reduced-calorie mayonnaise
¼   cup chopped fresh dill
4   oz smoked salmon, flaked
1   tsp mustard
Salt and pepper to taste
Fresh dill for garnish

Cut artichokes in half lengthwise and cut off points with scissors. Remove center petals and fuzzy centers. Cook orzo according to package instructions. Combine yogurt, mayonnaise, dill, and mustard. Add to cooked and drained orzo, and mix well. Gently stir in smoked salmon. Season with salt and pepper. Fill centers of prepared artichokes with pasta mixture. Garnish with springs of fresh dill.

Serves 4
Per serving: calories: 405   fat: 10 g

CHAPTER SIX

Eating on the Road Is a Piece of Cake

"We don't know what poor losers we are until we start dieting."

During the Manila International Film Festival with Jeremy Irons.

On location, on the set of *The Deep,* with Nick Nolte.

How to Survive a Cocktail Party

I have attended some of the most lavish cocktail parties in the world. Generally, they consist of drinks and assorted hot and cold finger foods, most of which are high in fat and calories!

Be prepared and you won't be trapped between the double-dipped, deep-fried cheeseballs and the spinach wrapped in butter-drenched phyllo dough. Before you leave your house, eat a few strawberries, a piece of melon, a salad, or some raw vegetables. This way you won't be famished when you arrive at the party. When I entertain, I always serve lots of delicious appetizers that are low in calories for my friends and the Star Dieters. However, if you find yourself at someone's home, who has not been thoughtful enough to consider the dieter, here are a few tips to get you through the night.

★ **1. Arrive fashionably late.** If the invitation says seven-thirty, arrive at eight-fifteen. Somebody has to be the first to arrive, but it doesn't have to be you. This way, you'll only have time for a drink or two and a few hors d'oeuvres.

★ **2. Check out the food table.** Eat only those foods that are low in calories such as crudités (raw vegetables). If there is something irresistible, take a small piece so that you don't feel deprived. Remember, you can get the full flavor of a food in just one, bite. If you can't eat just one, don't eat any. For example, you can allow yourself one spoonful of caviar, a single slice of smoked salmon on the world's tiniest piece of black bread, and a glass of champagne. Calories: 314. (Do be aware, however, that you've just eaten your dinner.)

★ **3. Don't stand near the food table.** Stand with your back to the food or on the other side of the room to avoid "unconscious" eating. Keep circulating and don't follow the handsome waiter around.

★ **4. Don't take a plate.** You'll be tempted to put too much food on it and eat too fast. Eat one hors d'oeuvre at a time.

★ **5. Beverages have calories, too!** Unless you choose low-calorie or calorie-free drinks (sparkling water, diet soda, tomato juice, etc), the calories in drinks can really add up! Limit your alcohol to two regular drinks, and then switch to something lighter such as a wine spritzer or watered-down mixed drinks with lots of ice. If someone offers to freshen your drink, say, "Thanks, all I need is more ice cubes."

★ **6. Dress for success.** If you look devastatingly gorgeous or breathtakingly handsome, you'll feel slim and sexy and will be less likely to blow it on a tray of bacon bites.

Remember, making new friends is dietetic.

HOW TO SURVIVE A COCKTAIL PARTY— DINNER INCLUDED

Should dinner be attached to the invitation, you still don't have to go off your diet. Banquets, charity events, and annual dinners are the worst challenges for the Star Dieter. You have little or no choice in what is served, and the menu is *always* high in calories.

If you have a choice of entrées, choose the least fattening and always ask that the sauce be served on the side. (And don't eat it!) Skip the potatoes, bread, and dessert. Pass on the sour cream, butter, sauces, gravy, and other fats. Eat half of your entrée, enjoy the vegetables and the salad without dressing, and flirt with everyone at the table.

Don't announce that you're on a diet. If the hostess tries to get you to eat more than you want, tell her, "I'm so full, I cannot eat another bite." If you can fake it without telling her, do it. (It's okay to lie a little here.) Otherwise, it will be the topic of conversation.

DINING OUT

From McDonald's to Burger King, airplane to amphitheater, sushi bar to salsa bar, Americans are eating out more than they ever have, and that includes cocktail parties, dinner parties, and restaurants. Nineties' lifestyles and two-income households have left fewer opportunities to eat at home. For business travelers, this means room service and meals-in-flight; for office workers and carpooling homemakers, it usually means eating at a fast-food restaurant. One recent government survey suggests that Americans average one meal on the road every day, and even more for children.

Whether it be a school cafeteria or a trendy night spot, any meal cooked by someone else is a dietary risk. Even a romantic night in an elegant restaurant has its pitfalls. After all, who can tell the difference between *au gratin* and mustard sauce in dim candlelight? Since there's no avoiding the problem, you might as well tackle it head on. With this in mind, I've plotted a map to help you through the mine field of fatty, high-calorie restaurant meals, to the relative safety of low-fat, high-carbohydrate home-made selections.

Fine Restaurants

If you're dining out, as most of us do either by design or necessity, you will have to learn how to *outwit the waiter*. Here are a few suggestions that pay off.

★   Choose a restaurant with a wide selection of low-calorie, low-fat foods that will accommodate your wishes.

★ Order an appetizer in place of an entrée. They are usually the right amount.

★ Ask that your food be prepared *exactly* the way you want it. For example, fish broiled without butter, vegetable steamed, no salt, dressing on the side.

★ Ask that the breadbasket be removed.

★ Ask that your food be served on a salad plate. This way half the entrée will fill the plate and give the illusion that you are eating the same amount as everyone else.

★ As soon as you're finished, ask that your plate be removed. It's better than regretting the fact that you've eaten more than you should. Never take a doggie bag home.

★ Finish the meal with a dish of fresh berries.

Bon appetit!

FAST FOODS

Burger Joints

When Burger King came up with the slogan "Have it your way," they were talking directly to the Star Dieter. A few commonsense selections can turn a high-calorie outing into a low-fat meal. What works well at Burger King will work equally well at McDonald's, Wendy's, Jack-in-the-Box, Taco Bell, etc. Even Domino's, Pizza Hut, and Kentucky Fried Chicken can be negotiated with a minimum of damage. Fortunately, the fast-food chains recognized a few years ago that unless they came up with a few healthier choices, they were in danger of losing a lot of health-conscious customers. You still have to choose carefully, but some surprisingly good choices are available.

Burger King.   To survive the fast-food wars, you must first know your enemies. Enemy number 1 is always the seductively tasty, greasy, and salty french fry. Generations of fast-food vendors have adopted the mantra, "Would you like fries with that?" Memorize this answer: "No!"

Enemy number 2 at every burger joint is the "Big Burger." Every restaurant has one; at Burger King, it's appropriately called the Whopper. At 711 calories and 35 percent fat, the Whopper with cheese is a heart attack in the making. Throw in 1,164 mg of sodium and 133 mg of cholesterol, and the picture is truly frightening.

There is some relief at Burger King for the protein-starved, however. Though not exactly on our daily diet, you can indulge yourself now and then with Chicken Tenders. At 204 calories and 10 grams of fat, Chicken Tenders deliver more meat and do less damage to your fat intake than their evil cousins, McDonald's Chicken McNuggets. Just remember that Chicken Tenders are a splurge, not a regular part of your diet.

McDonald's. When you're in the market for low-fat protein, McD.'s is definitely not the place. A McChicken Sandwich delivers 470 calories and 47 percent fat. The moral of this story: Don't order a sandwich at McDonald's. What you can order is their chicken fajita— at 185 calories and 8 grams of fat, it's a relatively healthy choice. If you must have a burger, go to the small hamburger, not too high in calories because of its size.

You can also satisfy your hunger pangs safely with their salad. The Chef Salad is heavy with fat, but the Chunky Chicken Salad is an excellent choice. With lite vinaigrette dressing this salad totals only 200 calories, 26 percent from fat. If you bring your own fat-free dressing, that total drops to 160 calories, only 20 percent from fat. Iced tea or Diet Coke complete your low-cal feast. If you simply must have dessert, go with a vanilla frozen yogurt cone. At 105 calories and 1 gram of fat for a 3 ounce cone, it's a pretty good bargain.

One last McWarning: Try not to sleepwalk under the golden arches at breakfast. The wildly popular Egg McMuffin, a combination of sausage, egg, and English muffin, has a stunning 505 calories of almost pure fat (60 percent, to be exact). It also contains 1,215 mg of sodium and 260 mg of cholesterol. By the time you've finished one, you might as well have stayed home and munched on a cube of salty butter. You can, however, purchase one of Ronald's no-fat muffins. The apple bran muffin, at 180 calories, and the blueberry muffin, at 170, are both good fat-free choices.

Wendy's. Wendy's mantra—"Where's the beef?"—made the chain an overnight sensation in the 1980s. Ironically, though, Wendy's has prospered in the long run by introducing a variety of low-fat, non beef items. Wendy's introduced the baked potato to the fast-food market and the first low-fat chicken breast sandwich. It was the first chain to expand their salad bar to include fruit and an extensive assortment of greens. For Star Dieters, Wendy's probably offers the greatest variety of low-fat choices of any of the hamburger chains.

A plain baked potato with salsa is an excellent choice at 270 calories and 0 fat. The grilled chicken fillet, eaten *without* the bun, is another safe choice at 100 calories. The salad bar offers a great selection, but watch out for the high-fat cheeses and dressings. Stick to the vegetables and fruit, and top your plate off with wine vinegar dressing.

As with any fast-food restaurant, though, you still have to be careful. Wendy's offers the usual "big burger" in the form of Wendy's Big Classic, 10 ounces of beef with 52 percent of its 570 calories from fat. Throw in another 70 calories for a slice of cheese, 30 for each strip of bacon, 90 for mayonnaise, and 71 for honey mustard sauce, and the Big Classic swells to an impressive 768 calories and 68 percent fat. Not exactly at the top of the Star Dieter's menu. Watch out for the Chicken Sandwich, as well. The fried variety, unlike the grilled, comes with 430 calories and its own supply of fat.

Pizza Parlors

Domino's and Pizza Hut. When you hear the word "pizza," you probably think "fat," but that isn't necessarily the case. The fat is in the cheese that usually goes on the pizza, not in the pizza itself. Pizza can actually be surprisingly nutritious; the flour, water, yeast, and baking soda in the crust, in fact, usually contain 0 fat. The tomato sauce globbed on top is also low-cal and low-fat. So far, so good. As long as you don't start loading on the cheese as well, you'll be all right. But remember, only one piece!.

"No cheese?" you ask. "Then what *do* I put on top?" I'm glad you asked. There are so many ways to top a pizza. Order yours with your low-cal favorites: green peppers, mushrooms, onions, eggplant, garlic, spinach, pineapple, and shrimp. And don't forget to ask for extra sauce. Most pizza restaurants will not only be willing, but delighted, to leave the cheese off at your request. After all, it's one of their most expensive ingredients. Order a cheese-free pizza and everybody wins. Just be sure you don't compensate for the missing cheese by adding a fatty substitute. You'll notice that pepperoni, sausage, anchovies, bacon, meatballs, and prosciutto are nowhere on my list of suggested toppings. They're nowhere on the Star Dieter's list at all.

Taco Stands

Taco Bell. Taco Bell offers a "light" alternative for its regular beef, taco shells, and cheese. The catch is, you have to request it at the time you order. Taco Bell also has a nutritional read-out available at the counter so you can find out exactly many calories you've bought before you chow down.

If you're going to eat Mexican, the operative word is "beans." Even though oil is added to the beans in refrying them, you can still get a reasonably low-fat bowl of beans with a sprinkling of grated cheese for under 200 calories. A crispy beef taco, though lower in calories (183), gets 54 percent of its calories from fat. The best choice for Star Dieters is a regular tostada without cheese. At 180 calories and 8 grams of fat, it's a low-fat winner. Do not, however, eat anything called "salad" at any of these places. The Taco Salad is a killer at 905 calories and 60 percent fat. So is anything labeled "supreme," which invariably means supremely high in fat from the sour cream and guacamole they've loaded on top.

Chicken Dinners

Kentucky Fried Chicken. No, it wasn't just a name change when the Colonel decided to start referring to his restaurants as KFC. It was a deliberate move to take the word "fried" out of people's consciousness. Since a single breast of Extra Crispy weighs in at 330 calories and over 50 percent fat, taking home a bucket means taking in enough fat for an Arctic winter. Fortunately, though, even the Colonel is now health-conscious enough to know that people want choices. The result is his new Tender Roast Chicken, seasoned with spices and cooked whole on a spit. You can order it by the piece, and if you have the fortitude to remove the crispy skin before you take a bite, you have a delicious, reasonably low-fat dinner. Your best choice is two-pieces of all-white with the skin removed. A 4 ounce serving has only 199 calories and 6 grams of fat. You might want to try the Colonel's vegetable medley salad (ask for the fat-free dressing) at 126 calories and 4 grams of fat, the small garden salad for 16 calories, or KFC's new mean greens (veggies) or green beans, all under 52 calories. Baked beans are another good selection at 132 calories and 2 grams of fat. Add a small serving of mashed potatoes at 70 calories and 1 gram of fat, or a serving of Garden Rice at 75 calories and 1 gram of fat, and you have a veritable feast. Dinner with the Colonel will still be finger-lickin' good, but you won't have hell to pay when you step on the scale the next day.

SPECIALTY RESTAURANTS

Chinese

Chinese food is served up in American towns from coast to coast— and that's a good thing for the Star Dieter. It is no coincidence that the Chinese population is blessed with low blood pressure and choles- terol, few weight problems, and an unusually low incidence of cancer and heart disease. The Chinese diet is one of the world's healthiest, and since it is entirely free of cheese products, it is a perfect choice for the Star Dieter. Nutritious and delicious, Chinese cooking is one of the best restaurant choices you can make.

Just as there are many dialects in the Chinese language, so are there many styles of Chinese cooking, each as distinct as the region in which it originated. The Southeast has produced Canton cuisine, fea- turing lots of roasted and grilled meats as well as shark fin and bird's nest soups. Fried rice is also a product of Cantonese cooking. The East Coast of China is responsible for Fukien cuisine. A New York favorite, Fukien cooking specializes in seafood and elaborate, delicious soups. Peking-Shantung cooking originated in the Northeast and is best known for Peking Duck and other elegant, refined dishes. The Central Hunan province is the originator of sweet-and-sour dishes, which come in dozens of versions. Finally, the Western region of China developed the hot and fiery Szechwan-Hunan pantry of spicy, low fat recipes.

In addition to these regional terms, Chinese cooking is often designated "Mandarin" or "Shanghai" as well. These are not regional descriptions; Mandarin is the Chinese word for "official" and usually means the food has been prepared according to time-honored traditions from all regions. Shanghai cooking, on the other hand, is China's *nouvelle cuisine,* reflecting the more modern, sophisticated dishes currently emerging in China's cities.

Unfortunately for Star Dieters, something seems to get lost in the translation when Americans sit down for a Chinese dinner. We manage to take a time-honored, low-fat cuisine and turn it into a traditionally American, fatty, salty feast. Instead of concentrating on the rice and noodle dishes as Chinese nationals do, Americans gorge on the meat and fish entrées. The minute a platter of General Tso's battered chicken hits the table, the person who ordered it starts eating directly from the serving plate, ignoring the empty plate set next to it for the individual's portion. We chow down on fried shrimp, fried egg rolls, and fried wonton's; bypass steamed rice in favor of fried. After porking out on breaded and fried sweet-and-sour dishes, we usually don't have room for the stir-fried vegetables. Instead of sharing entrées, with the entire table, we often eat the whole thing ourselves. And even when we do "share" high-calorie entrées, it's usually so everyone can have a "taste" of what everyone else has ordered.

The moral of this story is clear: Stop eating like an American, and start eating like a Chinese. The next time you're in a Chinese restaurant, watch a group of Chinese eat. They hold bowls of steamed rice close to their chins and occasionally add pieces of meat or fish from the central platter that everyone else at the table shares. They consume large amounts of steamed rice, lo mein noodles, fruit, and delicious vegetables like bok choy. Follow their example and turn your back on the fried rice, pan-fried noodles, and battered and fried goodies. Leave behind the sweet-and-sour items, drenched in sugar and fat (yes, even the spare ribs); ignore anything served in a "bird's nest" or fried (like egg foo young). Pass on the duck, which is served dripping with fat. Fill up on the steamed dishes, the fruits and vegetables, the hot-and-sour or sizzling rice soup. Bypass the green tea ice cream in favor of the pineapple chunks, lychee nuts (a wonderfully sweet fruit) or just the fortune cookie. You'll end a delicious meal with a crunchy cookie and a fortune that says, "You will succeed in your dietary endeavors."

Italian

Americans love Italian cooking. From pizza to pasta, calzone to cacciatore, it's wonderfully satisfying and scrumptiously good. Unfortunately, it can also be fattening. Order something drenched in cream and oil and piled with cheese, and you might as well order a double lard with extra cholesterol. *Mama mia!*

It is possible, however, to have a healthy, low-fat Italian meal. The key is to understand how Italians themselves actually eat. In Italy, the main meal of the day is lunch. To give themselves time for this meal, Italians still maintain the custom (maddening to Americans) of shutting down their stores and shops for two hours smack in the middle of every day. Because the meal is so large, it is served in courses, beginning with antipasto. The typical antipasto consists of cold meat and cheese, fried mozzarella sticks, and soup—hot minestrone or *pasta e fagioli* (pasta and bean). The antipasto is followed by the *primo piatto,* typically a small serving of plain pasta, accompanied by the *secondo piatto,* the meat or seafood course. These are followed by the *insalata,* the salad course, intended to cleanse the palate and prepare you for the final course of espresso and *biscotto.*

Needless to say, few Americans have time for these two-hour lunches. When we eat Italian, we usually have a large evening meal centered around pasta. Now this isn't necessarily a bad thing. Although pasta has received a great deal of bad press, the humble noodle is actually quite low in fat and calories. It's the amount we eat or what we pile on top of or stuff inside the pasta that gets us in trouble. Alfredo sauce, apparently named after a man with a death wish, is a combination of cream, cheese, and fat. Carbonara sauce is a blend of cream, eggs, cheese, and bacon; pesto sauce combines basil with pine nuts, cheese, and oil. All these sauces are lethal to the Star Dieter.

You also need to watch out for fatty Italian meats and cheeses. This means steering clear of lasagna (meat and four cheeses), ravioli, tortellini, manicotti, and cannelloni (stuffed with meat or cheese). You'll also want to avoid saltimbocca (veal sautéed in butter and topped with prosciutto), prosciutto (thinly sliced ham), and pancetta (Italian bacon). Anything heaped with cheese is also out, though you can certainly treat yourself to a sprinkling of parmesan, made from skim milk. Even here, though, remember when to say "when."

The other two big "no-no's" in Italian restaurants are risotto and bread. Just mention the word "risotto" and you'll really get me going. It's the newest rage in the best Italian restaurants. Having discovered how much Americans love rice, the Italians have obliged us with a short-grain variety, creamed with cheese and butter. Everyone loves it—who wouldn't? It's incredibly delicious, and nearly all fat. The other dieter's nightmare, bread, entices you with its crispy crust and soft center. It simply screams to be slathered with butter or drizzled with olive oil. Unless you have nerves of steel, have the waiter place the bread basket as far away from you as possible. Better yet, tell him not to leave it at all.

By now you're thinking, but what's left? Fortunately, lots of things. Pasta itself is a good choice, and these days it seems to come in infinite varieties. The most common are angel hair, linguine, fettucini, ziti, fusilli, and of course, spaghetti. Pile on some marinara, tomato and basil, cacciatore, or primavera sauce. (Make sure the primavera sauce hasn't had cream added.) All these sauces are vegetable based, with no meat and little or no fat. They will add nothing but fabulous flavor to your meal. Sprinkle on a little parmesan cheese, and you have a delicious and satisfying meal. You can also order plain risotto, seasoned with vegetables and herbs only. Salad is always a great choice, as long as you don't add fatty dressings. And for dessert, bypass the spumoni, cannoli, tortoni, and gelati in favor of a premium, cup of Italian coffee. From espresso to cappuccino, these delicious blends can be accented with a touch of Kahlua, Amaretto, or other wonderful liqueur if you're really feeling wild. *Delizioso!*

Greek

Zorba already knew something that Americans are just beginning to figure out. Greek food is sensational, and over the last five years, it has become easier and easier to find it in the good old United States. Though it's not yet as popular as Chinese, Italian, or Mexican, it's well on its way to every city and hamlet in America. For Star Dieters there are plenty of good choices, but since you may not be familiar with Greek cuisine, I'll take you through the ordering process one course at a time.

Consider starting with a salad instead of a rich appetizer. The Greek salads *(salates)* are an excellent way to begin your meal. A typical house salad mixes cucumbers, tomatoes, green peppers, onions, olives, feta cheese, and yogurt dressing. A second salad choice is the *horta,* or "hot" salad. Endive is boiled in lemon water to which olive oil has been added, and the salad is then served warm. Whichever salad you order, however, watch out for the feta and olives. Both will drive the fat and sodium content through the roof.

Let's begin with the appetizers: lentil soup, low-fat and incredibly light, is an excellent starter. Tabbouleh, made of bulgur, finely chopped onions, tomatoes, cucumbers, parsley, fresh mint, olive oil, and lemon also makes a fine starter as long as the chef isn't heavy-handed with the oil. Foods that signal high fat in the appetizer course include spanakopita, a flaky phyllo crust interlaced with spinach and feta cheese. It looks light enough, but when you know that each sheet of phyllo is spread with butter to give it that wonderful puff, you'll know why you should avoid it. Also dangerous are the heavyweight *keftadakia* (Greek meatballs), *louganiko* (Greek sausage), and *kalamaria* (deep-fried squid). *Avgolemono,* a popular Greek soup blending chicken, rice, egg, and lemon, is also out of the Star Dieter's fat range.

On to the main course. *Moussaka* is the national dish of Greece. Prepared with ground lamb and beef, layered with slices of eggplant and zucchini, and topped with a *béchamel* sauce made of butter, flour, and milk, it is high in fat. *Avoid* it. A much better choice for Star Dieters is *psari plaki,* a filet of white fish with sliced potatoes, tomatoes, bell peppers, and olives. If you're in the mood for meat, an excellent choice is *gernista,* bell peppers stuffed with lamb, beef, rice, and onions. The accent is usually on the rice and onions, which keeps the fat content low. Another choice would be *souvlaki,* more commonly known as shish-kebab. By the time you get the broiled meat off the sticks and into your mouth, your stomach has had time to catch up with your appetite.

The final course is dessert, headlined by the famous *baklava,* a dieter's nightmare made of phyllo pastry, butter, honey, nuts, and spices. Don't even look at it. Instead, go for a cup of Greek coffee, which is even stonger than espresso and guaranteed to leave you hanging from the ceiling.

One last warning: The Greeks are BIG eaters, and I do mean big. No matter what you order, you may end up with too much food, especially considering that most main courses come with side dishes of rice, vegetables, salad, and pita bread. You'll be better off by passing the meals and ordering à la carte.

Mexican

It's no surprise that Mexican food has crossed the northern border. Even if Mexico wasn't located so conveniently close, the delicious, spicy foods native to our southern neighbor would have found their way into middle America. One reason is the millions of Americans of Mexican ancestry. A bigger reason is the food itself. No one will be surprised to hear that Mexican food is the most popular ethnic cuisine in the United States.

Unfortunately, when most of us think "Mexican," we picture nacho chips covered with melted cheese, jalapeños, and mounds of sour cream. Clearly, this is not an acceptable choice for the Star Dieter. Neither is the *quesadilla* (tortillas stuffed with cheese and dripping with fat), the *chili con queso* (cheese melted with green chile peppers), the refried beans that have been loaded with lard, or the guacamole and deep-fried chips. This is not news to you. You already know these dishes are awash with fat and salt. You also know you must avoid the deep-fried *chimichangas* (rolled tortillas filled with meat, chicken, or shrimp) and the *flautas con crema* (chimichangas topped with spicy cream). Anything fried, cheesed, or sour creamed is automatically forbidden.

What's left? Lots of good things. Low fat, nutritious choices can be made in any Mexican restaurant. For an appetizer, bypass the nachos in favor of a Mexican salad. I'm talking about *salad,* not the tostada sometimes listed as one of the salad choices. True Mexican salad is a mixture of lettuce, onions, and quartered tomatoes topped with salsa. If you're not in the mood for salad, begin your meal with Soup a Mexicana. Good low-fat choices are chilled gazpacho (made of chopped tomatoes and onions) or warm black bean soup.

When you're ready to move on to the main course, consider *fajitas,* a delicious selection of grilled beef, chicken, or shrimp, served with an assortment of vegetables. Many restaurants these days let you assemble your own at the table. Bean burritos are also an acceptable choice, especially at the many restaurants that no longer prepare them with lard; just ask them to hold the cheese. *Arroz con pollo* (chicken fillet atop spicy rice, served with a vegetable sauce) or *camarones de hacha* (shrimp sautéed in a red and green tomato/coriander sauce) are also excellent choices. For side dishes, Mexican rice, black beans, and tortillas with salsa are also acceptable, as long as you limit the quantities.

As with Greek food, let me offer you a final warning: Do not, I repeat, do not, avail yourself of the national dessert of Mexico— *sopaipillas.* These wickedly delicious little pastries are actually "pillows" of dough, deep-fried and then covered? with powdered sugar or honey. One or two of these "light" pastries is guaranteed to plug every artery you have. Better to have another bowl of rice or an extra tortilla. Consider them damage control.

Japanese

Truman Capote once told me that a visit to an authentic Japanese restaurant is more therapeutic than a session with a therapist. I couldn't agree with him more. The key word in Japan's culture is "harmony" and it extends not only to their way of life but to their food as well. Japanese food is an art form. The aim is to create a presentation of healthful delicacies that will soothe the soul, delight the eye, and nourish the body. Incredibly, the Japanese succeed in doing this time and again.

Since the islands of Japan are surrounded by water, fish plays a major part in the country's cooking heritage. Rice, grown in Japan's water paddies, is the second staple of the Japanese diet. With land at such a premium in this small nation, grazing cattle is prohibitive. The result is a diet virtually free of beef and cheese (unless you wander into a Benihana steakhouse!). The absence of cattle and their dietary by-products has produced a nutritious, low-fat way of eating that has kept the Japanese people almost free of heart attacks and given them one of the lowest disease rates in the world. Westerners have a lot to learn from the Japanese way of eating.

Traditional Japanese restaurants are a boon to Star Dieters. The typical menu is replete with appetizers such as delicious low-fat soups—*miso* and *udon* noodle are excellent choices—and with salads such as *sunomono* or *aemono,* both based on a selection of fresh seaweeds. For a main course try *shumai*—steamed shrimp dumplings wrapped in noodle skin—or *teriyaki*—chicken, beef, or shellfish marinated in a soy mixture that includes sugar, ginger, and sake. Teriyaki is usually low in fat, though it may be high in sodium. *Sukiyaki,* another good choice, is stir-fried bits of meat, chicken, and shrimp mixed with vegetables, flavored with soy sauce, and cooked together as a single dish. Also consider *yosenabe* (noodles and seafood simmered in broth).

The trendiest of the current Japanese dishes, of course, are *sushi* and *sashimi,* which include raw fish among their ingredients. Serving raw fish either rolled or filleted is big business in both Japan and America. Though it isn't my favorite, there's no doubt it was the yuppie delicacy of the eighties and nineties. Contrary to popular belief, *sushi* doesn't always include raw fish. Sushi is the result of marinating boiled, short-grain rice in sweetened rice vinegar, rolling it in seaweed sheets called *nori,* and then cutting the rolls into bite-size portions. Sometimes raw fish is added to the sushi roll or placed on top of the vinegared rice (called *nigiri sushi).* At other times vegetables, pickles, or tofu are rolled with the rice.

Sashimi, on the other hand, is always raw fish. Arranged in small dishes, sashimi, like sushi, is served with a touch of *wasabi* (a green Japanese horseradish) and soy sauce for dipping. A little bit of *wasabi* goes a long way for most Americans. For that matter, so does sashimi. Although the portions are small, be careful how much you order. In Japanese restaurants, less is often more—both sushi and sashimi carry hefty price tags.

When it comes to ordering any form of raw fish, be very, very cautious. Although raw fish is low-fat, high-protein, and very trendy, it can also be dangerous. The United States Department of Agriculture has issued a warning that *sashimi* may contain the parasitic round-worm *anisakis*. The disease you may contract is called *anisakiasis* by the medical community. Believe me, you'll know if you have it. Your stomach and bowels will be complaining for days and days, not to mention the psychological effects of knowing there's a worm in your system. The bottom line on eating sushi and sashimi is to know your source. The more popular the restaurant, the less likely that people have been getting sick there. Still, you eat your fish, you take your chances. If you must eat it, keep your fingers crossed.

While you're at it, there are a few other foods you should avoid. They won't send you to the hospital (at least not right away!), but they will drive your fat count sky-high. Anything labeled "tempura" has been dipped in batter and fried in fat. No matter what the "dippee" is, avoid it. *Agemono* also means deep-fried, so cross it off your list. *Shabu-shabu*—sliced beef and veggies served with noodles—is also off-limits.

Happily, a Japanese restaurant is one of the few places you can order dessert with a clear conscience. The always respectful Japanese would never think of insulting your stomach with a gooey, rich concoction after such a healthy meal. Instead, they will offer you a tray of sweet fruits cut in such a variety of designs that you'll swear there's magic involved. There is.

French

For years the French seemed to have the inside track on elegant dining. If you heard the words "fancy restaurant," you automatically filled in the word "French." French food was America's first official "foreign food." It's been here since the days of the French and Indian War. Though the French lost the war, they left their recipe books behind as they hightailed it back to the Continent.

"Fancy" isn't the only word that comes to mind when we think of French cooking. We also think of heavy cream sauces and mounds of fat. For many years that reputation was justified, but in recent years things have begun to change. When one too many customers dropped dead of a coronary, those snooty French chefs finally stopped laughing at the concept of low-fat cooking and began thinking, *"C'est possible?"* The result was *nouvelle cuisine,* an elegant term meaning "new cooking," which offers the diet-conscious a much healthier selection of menu choices.

Even so, the menu in a French restaurant remains a dieter's minefield and the attitude of the waiters, who deign only to intimidate, is another obstacle to be overcome. Nevertheless, if you are going to eat French at all, you must gather your courage and stick to your guns.

Read the food descriptions carefully. If the menu says a selection is grilled, poached, broiled, roasted, boiled, blackened, marinated, or steamed, chances are you're on safe ground. But if it says *au gratin,* stuffed, hollandaise, *crème fraîche, saucisse, buerre,* butter, or bacon, run for your life.

Tell your waiter you want your entrée prepared without oil or butter, your vegetables steamed and served plain. Your waiter will undoubtedly tell you (with eyebrows raised) that it is simply *impossible*. He will assure you that it cannot be done, and besides, he can assure you that *monsieur et madame* will never gain an ounce.

Don't you believe him. Insist on having your food prepared the way you want it, and make it clear that the choices are accommodating you or showing you to the door. Even the snootiest waiter will usually give in and discover it is *possible* after all.

Now down to the specifics. When it comes to appetizers, avoid both the creamed and the French onion soup. Creamed soup is butter-based and the onion soup is high in sodium and loaded with cheeses. Choose a clear broth or consommé with vegetables instead.

If you prefer salad, you'll have plenty of trendy, shriveled, rather bitter-tasting greens to choose from. You might want to select one of the tricolor salads made of radicchio, endive, and arugula. Jicama and watercress are also good choices. Almost all are dietetically acceptable, though not always as tasty as you might hope. The danger comes not with the greens, but with the toppings. There is no such thing as low-cal dressing in a French restaurant. The French love to include bacon in their salads, either in bacon bits or as part of the dressing. Even oil and vinegar are a risk, since the French are long on oil and short on vinegar. The best you can do besides taking your own (and I do) is to ask for a cruet of balsamic vinegar. It's delicious, low-calorie—

and Italian! Watch out for those homemade croutons as well. Like nearly everything else in France, they've been sautéed in butter.

Ordering your entrée is tricky as well. Besides taking a good look at the way it's prepared, be cautious about ordering veal, duck, and lamb, three items which the French seem to think they invented. The exception would be *nouvelle cuisine* restaurants, where they sometimes prepare paper-thin slices of all three meats served with a fruit or herb sauce. Since not all French restaurants offer these, ask before you order.

Also be cautious when ordering vegetables. If you don't request otherwise, your meal is likely to show up with a vegetable that's been buttered, creamed, and puréed within an inch of its life. This is one of those times when you'll have to be firm with your waiter.

As for dessert, it's pretty much out of the question. The French are notorious for their rich pastries and desserts. It's a reputation they've built on the graves of countless fat people. There's simply no way even to taste a French dessert without gaining five pounds. It's in the accent; just saying "chantilly" or "crème fraîche" is fattening. If you simply must put something in your mouth during the dessert course as protection against temptation, ask for a small bowl of raspberries *au naturel.* Your waistline will thank you.

AIRLINE FOOD

Long the bane of the health-conscious (or anyone with taste buds), airlines in America are finally cleaning up their dietary act. According to an Alaska Airlines chairman, "There's a revolution underway in America's stomachs. More and more people are turning away from heavy food, opting for lighter fare." Alaska Airline's had made efforts to lighten the weight airborne.

Alaska, American, and other prominent U.S. airlines are more frequently offering meals that emphasize grilled meats (including skinless white chicken) and forgo rich sauces. American Airlines serve Weight Watchers entrées as part of their regular in-flight menu on transcontinental flights and as a special meal request on all domestic flights. All the airlines are making efforts to cut the amount of fat and cholesterol in their in-flight meals. Even the beverage cart is more calorie-friendly, with diet and club sodas as standard items. Fewer hard liquors and liqueurs are offered, and the selection of wines has increased. Champagne, happily, is still available. Though foreign carriers still lag behind in the effort to clean up their dietary act, even there we see a steady trend toward lower-fat, lower-calorie meals.

Whether you're taking a U.S. or foreign carrier, however, it's best not to leave your meal selection to chance. Since it's impossible to be certain which meals will be offered on your particular flight, it's safest to call in a special meal order at least 24 hours in advance.

The following charts list the special meal choices available on the various airlines. The selection is impressive. The airlines have clearly made an attempt, collectively and individually, to meet the dietary needs of their customers, whether for health or religious reasons. Take advantage of these offerings. They really are something special in the air.

U.S. Carriers

Special Meals	Alaska	America West	American	Continental	Delta	Northwest	TWA	United	USAir
Baby		x		x	x	x		x	x
Bland	x		x		x	x		x	x
Children	x	x		x	x	x	x	x	x
Diabetic	x	x	x	x	x	x		x	x
Fruit	x	x		x	x	x		x	x
Gluten-Free			x		x	x		x	x
High-Fiber									x
High-Protein									x
Hindu			x		x	x		x	x
Kosher	x	x	x	x	x	x	x	x	x
Lactose-Free			x					x	x
Lacto-Vegetarian	x	x	x	x	x	x		x	x
Low-Calorie	x		x		x	x	x	x	x
Low-Carbohydrate			x			x	x	x	
Low-Fat/Cholesterol	x	x	x	x	x	x	x	x	x
Low-Fiber	x								
Low-Protein									x
Low-Purine									x
Low-Sodium		x	x		x	x	x	x	x
Moslem			x	x	x	x		x	x
Oriental					x	x		x	x
Seafood	x			x	x	x	x	x	x
Vegetarian-Vegan	x	x	x	x	x	x	x	x	x

International Carriers

Special Meals	Air France	Alitalia	ANA - All Nippon	Air Canada	British Airways	Cathay Pacific	China Airlines	El Al Airlines	Finnair	Iberia Airlines	Japan Airlines	KLM Royal Dutch Airlines	Korean Airlines	Lufthansa German Airlines	Olympic Airways	SAS Scandinavian Airlines	Singapore Airlines	Swissair	Varig Brazilian airlines	Virgin Atlantic
Baby	x				x	x	x				x	x				x				
Bland	x			x	x				x	x	x		x	x		x				
Children	x				x	x	x	x			x	x				x			x	x
Diabetic	x	x	x	x	x	x	x	x	x	x	x	x	x	x		x	x	x	x	x
Fruit		x	x	x		x			x	x				x		x	x			
Gluten-Free				x	x	x			x	x	x	x	x	x			x	x	x	
High-Fiber					x	x	x		x		x	x		x			x		x	
High-Protein																				
Hindu	x	x	x		x		x	x	x	x	x	x	x	x	x	x	x	x	x	x
Kosher	x	x	x	x	x	x	x	x	x	x	x	x	x	x	x	x	x	x	x	x
Lactose-Free					x				x	x				x	x	x			x	
Lacto-Vegetarian	x	x		x	x				x	x	x	x	x			x		x	x	
Low-Calorie		x	x	x	x	x	x	x	x	x	x	x	x	x	x	x	x	x	x	
Low-Carbohydrate																				
Low-Fat/Cholesterol	x	x	x	x	x	x	x	x	x	x	x	x	x	x	x	x	x	x	x	x
Low-Fiber					x															
Low-Protein					x	x	x		x		x			x						
Low-Purine					x				x		x				x	x				
Low-Sodium	x	x	x	x	x	x	x	x	x	x	x	x	x	x	x	x	x	x	x	x
Moslem	x		x		x	x	x	x	x	x	x	x	x	x	x	x	x	x	x	x
Oriental	x				x	x			x	x	x			x		x		x		
Seafood	x	x		x	x		x	x	x	x	x			x	x	x		x	x	x
Vegetarian-Vegan	x	x	x	x	x	x	x	x	x	x	x	x		x	x	x	x	x	x	x

CHAPTER SEVEN

Star Light, Star Bright, What Do I Eat Tonight?

"He who indulges—bulges."

Scott Downie/Celebrity Photo Agency

Jill St. John, Michelle Lee, me, and Beverly D´Angelo in Beverly Hills.

At a Halloween party with Milton Berle.

While other girls were joining the Scouts, I was packing myself off to spas. At the time they preferred the euphemism "retreat," hoping to make the unwary believe they weren't really going off to diet boot camp. It didn't matter to me; as far as I was concerned, they could strap me to a wall. All I wanted was to go away for a week and come back thinner—a new and improved me. I didn't care how they did it.

In the years that have followed, I've continued to make the rounds from spa to spa, dropping pounds and inches at a good two dozen of the finest establishments of health and beauty. From Baden-Baden, Germany, to Ka'a'awa, Hawaii; from St. Moritz, Switzerland, to Oconomowoc, Wisconsin, to Vista, California, I've been pummeled, aerobicized, motivated, plunged, soothed, smoothed, and pampered. I've been fed low-calorie gourmet meals by the celebrated chefs of the rich and famous. And I've learned a lot along the way.

Each and every spa experience offered me a new insight into the fight to stay trim. Because I've always considered myself a great cook, I made a point to pay attention to the culinary masterpieces presented to me. I knew that if I could master the art of cooking correctly, I would have the insight I needed to maintain the figure I had on the day I left the spa. I gradually came to realize that my "great cooking" was actually a nutritional time bomb designed to explode into fat cells. I had to change my ways, and I was determined to learn from the best. Because I'm a natural snoop, I soon made it a point to become fast friends with the chef at every spa I visited. Eventually, he or she would share some of the spa's best secrets. Along the way I learned that no two spas are alike.

The Ashram, in Calabasas, California, takes the hard-nosed approach. Rather than preparing gourmet delights, they feed you next to nothing and make everyone dress alike in unflattering red sweat suits. The Belmilon Beauty and Fitness Spa, housed inside the Grand Hotel Beau Rivage in Interlaken, Switzerland, takes the opposite approach. Housed in an atmosphere of elegance and extravagance, you sink into the lap of luxury as they finesse the pounds away. Nearby, at Clinic La Prairie in Montreux, I was injected with the cells of a black sheep, a mysterious ritual purported to melt the pounds away.

In Paris I shared a fruit compote with a dieting ex–Secretary of State at the Hotel Ritz Health Club, and had my lymph drained at the nearby Royal Monceau's Les Thermes (though not on the same day!). Italy afforded me the chance to be submerged in volcanic mud at the Grand Hotel Orologio in Abano Terme, a ritual Ronald Reagan also decided to try. A stop at the San Souci Hotel Club and Spa in Ocho Rios, Jamaica, gave me the chance to drop a few pounds by dancing the night away.

Not to be outdone by their European counterparts, the Americas offered me a chance to tone in luxury closer to home. I biked with a Catholic bishop in Tecate, Mexico's, Rancho La Puerta, and I walked through a wrong door and stumbled onto a hush-hush meeting between two towel-wrapped U.S. senators at the Spa at Turnberry Isle in North Miami Beach. It was on the opposite coast, at Two Bunch Palms in Desert Hot Springs, California, that I witnessed the introduction of a famous singing star to an equally famous gigolo. I told you I'm a snoop.

But of all the spas I've visited in my world tours, my two favorites have to be the legendary Golden Door in Escondido, California, and the incredible Cal-a-Vie, in Vista, California. Entering the Golden Door is like slipping into another world of gentle relaxation. You leave the real world behind as you sink into the ambiance of the Japanese teahouse atmosphere. Everything, right down to the food, is exquisite. Even the vegetables are carefully carved and arranged as works of art.

Just as the Golden Door gently echoes Oriental tranquillity, so the Doral Saturnia evokes Europe in the middle of Miami Beach. The spa's lush formal gardens, Tuscany roofs, and Botticelli-like murals in the lobby reflect the Italian influence. Inside is a beauty salon called the Institute di Saturnia, where pampering has been raised to an art form. The Golden Door, the Doral Saturnia, and my favorite, Cal-a-Vie, leave you feeling relaxed, refreshed, and rejuvenated. The *piéce de résistance* of all this indulgence is a slimmer, firmer figure.

My world travels paid off not only in a newer, better me, but in a collection of recipes unequaled anywhere. First—and for the first time—I've gathered the secret recipes from the world's most famous spas together in a single collection with the blessings of the chefs who invented them. Each one is a masterpiece of fine dining with a minimum of fat and calories. Second, some of my celebrity friends have contributed personal recipes as well. And finally, as a crowning touch, the chefs at several restaurants favored by these celebrities have also shared a few of their cooking secrets.

I caution you that some of the ingredients in these recipes may not always be low-fat or low-calorie. I decided to include the original recipes, without any modification, so that you can see how the stars really eat (sometimes!) and what they really like.

However, you can easily incorporate these fabulous recipes into your diet plan with just a few minor modifications. I have included a list of ingredient substitutions that greatly cut the calories and fat without changing the taste.

Have a great time dining with the stars!

EASY RECIPE SUBSTITUTIONS

Substitute the following healthful ingredients for higher-fat, higher-calorie ingredients, without sacrificing taste in your favorite recipes.

Instead of:	*Substitute:*
butter or margarine in baking	equal amount of applesauce (or prune purée)
butter or margarine for spread	fat-free margarine, apple butter, lite margarine

cheddar cheese	lite or fat-free sharp cheddar cheese
cream	evaporated skim milk
cream to thicken soup	potato purée or half low-fat milk and half fat-free whipped cream
cream cheese	lite or fat-free cream cheese; Neufchâtel
egg, 1 whole	2 egg whites
evaporated milk	evaporated skim milk
gravy	packaged gravy mixes or fat-free bottled gravy
oil or butter for sautéing	fat-free chicken or vegetable broth
salad dressing	fat-free salad dressing; flavored vinegars (raspberry, balsamic, Italian seasoned wine vinegar) or fresh-squeezed lemon juice, Nikki's All-Purpose Dressing
sour cream	low-fat or non-fat yogurt or sour cream For dips: blended fat-free cottage cheese or fat-free ricotta cheese
whole milk	skim or 1% milk
chopped nuts	water chestnuts
high-fat sauce over fish, poultry	Nikki's All-Purpose Dressing

RECIPES FROM SPAS AND RESORTS

The Golden Door

ESCONDIDO, CA

The Golden Door is America's ultimate spa, costing approximately $5,000 per week. Every week a small group of women arrive on Sunday. They are weighed, measured, exercised, massaged, and fed the right food to keep slim and trim.

Greek Avgolemono Soup

1   egg
1½   tbsp fresh lemon juice
2   cups chicken broth (recipe below)
grated lemon peel
minced parsley or fresh mint for garnish

In a bowl, blend egg and lemon juice. Heat broth until boiling. Remove from heat. Beat small amount of the hot broth into the eggs, then add to remaining broth, beating constantly. Reheat, continuing to stir constantly. Serve hot. Sprinkle one or more of the garnishes on top.

Serves two
Per servings: 160 calories   fat: 8g

Golden Door Basic Broth

2   quarts water
1   3-pound roasting chicken
5   carrots, peeled and cut in chunks
5   stalks of celery
3   onions
5   cloves
5   peppercorns
1   tsp thyme
3   cloves garlic
parsley to taste

Be sure to wash the chicken before putting it in a large pot. Add the water and other ingredients and bring to a boil. Boil for 30 minutes, removing the scum that floats on the surface of the pot. Turn down heat and simmer a minimum of 4 hours. Use a colander lined with cheesecloth to strain.

Yield: 7 cups
Per one cup serving: 50 calories   fat: 1.5 g

Brenner's Park Hotel & Spa

BADEN-BADEN

The exclusive Brenner's Park Hotel in Baden-Baden sent me one of their recipes. The daily menu at this Spa totals 1,000 calories.

Fillet of Sole with Cucumber, Tomato, and Basil

2	tomatoes
6	oz cucumber
1	shallot
1	tsp light margarine
½	cup white wine
salt and pepper to taste	
1	tsp fresh basil
4–5	oz fillet of sole
½	cup potatoes, steamed
2	cups lettuce

Dice the tomatoes and place them in cooking water until you can peel them. Peel, divide, and cut the cucumber and remove the kernels.

Cut the shallot and place it in a pan with the margarine. Steam the cucumber and the tomatoes in the same pan, adding the white wine, salt, and pepper, and simmer until cucumber is soft. Before serving the vegetable, add one spoonful of fresh basil.

Put the sole with salt and lemon juice into a pan and fry it on both sides. Serve it together with ½ cup steamed potatoes or 2 cups of lettuce.

Serves 4
Per serving: calories: 400 fat: 2 g

Cal-A-Vie, The Ultimate Spa

VISTA, CA

Cal-a-Vie is an elite, secluded spa on 150 woodsy acres north of San Diego. It boasts wonderful food, great beauty treatments, and enough seaweed wraps to suit a mermaid!

Eggplant Rollatini with Spinach and Cheese Filling

FILLING:

2	large onions, finely chopped
2	large cloves garlic, minced
1	tsp olive oil
1½	lb fresh spinach (approx. 7 bunches) or substitute 30 oz frozen spinach, thawed
5	ounces feta cheese
1½	lbs low-fat cottage cheese or extra-skim ricotta
⅓	cup walnuts, coarsely chopped
1	whole egg
3	egg whites
2	tbsp parsley, minced
2	tbsp fresh basil, minced
1½	cups dry whole wheat bread crumbs (6–7 slices, dried)
2	tsp freshly ground black pepper
¼	tsp ground nutmeg or mace
½	tsp ground fennel or cumin seed

ROLLATINI:

4	medium eggplants (1½ lb each)
2	tsp olive oil
3	cups fresh tomato sauce

GARNISH:

12	**pitted black olives, sliced**
2	**tbsp grated Parmesan cheese**
4	**tbsp minced parsley**

Sauté onions and garlic in olive oil until softened. Add destemmed, chopped spinach and cook until wilted. Remove from heat and let cool slightly. Add the cheeses, nuts, eggs, parsley, basil, and spices. Set aside.

Peel eggplants if desired, and thinly slice lengthwise. Place slices on cookie sheets and lightly brush with olive oil. Cook in broiler as far from the heat as possible until just lightly browned. Remove from broiler and immediately cover pan with plastic wrap to allow eggplant to continue steaming.

Once cool, fill each eggplant slice with 2–3 tbsp of the spinach mixture, placing filling at the narrow end, then rolling up. Place in a baking dish, with seam facing down. Pour tomato sauce over the top of each rollatini and bake in a 375 ° degree oven until tomato sauce is bubbling—approximately 20–25 minutes.

Before serving, garnish with black olive slices and a sprinkling of Parmesan cheese and parsley. Serve with a large mixed green salad with non fat dressing and a slice of whole grain baguette to create a balanced meal.

Serves 10
Per serving: calories: 310   fat: 9. 5 g

Gurney's Inn:
The International Health and Beauty Spa
MONTAUK, NEW YORK

Shrimp with Stir-Fried Vegetables

1   carrot
1   head of broccoli
½   head of cauliflower
½   lb mushroom
1   lb shrimp
1   tbsp safflower oil
1   bunch scallions
1   tsp garlic
2   tsp basil (fresh)
2   oz white wine
black pepper to taste

Steam vegetables to al dente. Sauté shrimp in oil, add scallions, garlic, basil, and white wine. Add carrot, broccoli, cauliflower, and mushrooms and season with black pepper to taste.

Serves 4
Per serving: calories: 215 fat: 6 g

The Greenhouse Spa
ARLINGTON, TX

Vegetable Chili

1	cup dried lentils
1	cup dried pinto beans
1	cup dried small navy beans
1	cup dried black beans
1½	tsp olive oil
2	cups carrots, finely diced
1	cup celery, finely diced
¾	cups onion, finely chopped
¾	cups green pepper, finely chopped
2	medium cloves garlic, minced
1	tsp salt
1	tsp cumin
3	tbsp chili powder
1	tbsp sugar
¾	tsp crushed red pepper
2	cups tomato sauce
¼	cups chili paste

Sort beans, removing stones and/or debris. Rinse and place in a large stock pot, cover with cold water, and soak overnight.

Heat large stock pot; add olive oil, heat, and tilt pot to evenly coat with oil. Add carrots, celery, onion, pepper, garlic, salt, cumin, chili powder, sugar, and crushed red pepper. Sauté, stirring frequently.

Drain and rinse beans. Add to vegetables along with 1 gallon of water and tomato sauce. Bring to a boil, reduce heat, simmer for 4 hours, stirring occasionally. Serve hot.

Serves 12
Per serving: calories: 160 fat: 1 g

The Oaks At Ojai

OJAI, CA

Oriental Rice Salad

2 cups brown rice, cooked
1 cup mushrooms, sliced
1 cup snow peas or edible pea pods
1 cup celery, sliced thin on a diagonal
½ cup red bell peppers, slivered
½ cup scallions, minced

Combine and toss lightly.

1 tbsp sesame oil
¼ cup rice vinegar
2 tbsp low-sodium soy sauce

Combine and mix well. Toss dressing with rice mixture and chill.

¼ cup almonds toasted and slivered

Serves 8
Per serving: calories: 115   fat: 4 g

The Palms at Palm Springs
PALM SPRINGS, CA

The Palms Chicken Supreme

12	skinless chicken breasts, poached or roasted
1½	cups mushrooms, sliced
¼	tsp dill weed, dried and crushed
½	cup onion, chopped fine
1	tbsp lemon juice, fresh
12	oz mozzarella, sliced thin
½	cup Parmesan cheese, grated
1	tbsp paprika

Cut each breast in half and then slit half-breast sideways to prepare for stuffing. Combine mushrooms, dill weed, onion, and lemon juice, and stuff in the slit chicken breasts. Insert half of the mozzarella in the chicken breasts and the remaining half on top of the chicken pieces. Combine and sprinkle the Parmesan and paprika over the chicken. Bake at 400° until the top of each piece browns and the mozzarella melts.

Serves 24
Per serving (3 oz chicken breast): calories: 135 fat: 5 g

The Palms Cheesy Sea Bass

6	tbsp butter or margarine, melted
1½	cups Parmesan cheese
¾	cup yellow corn meal
¾	cup whole wheat flour
1½	tbsp black pepper
1	tbsp paprika (Spanish if available)
6	snapper, cod, or ocean perch fillets

Pour melted butter/margarine into a flat baking pan. Combine the Parmesan, cornmeal, flour, pepper, and paprika in a paper bag. Place 4-oz fillets in the bag and shake to coat each fillet. Place fish in baking pan and turn once to coat with butter. *Do not soak the fish in butter, just coat lightly.* Pour the remaining cheese-cornmeal-flour mixture onto the fish. Bake at 400° for approximately 20 minutes until the fish is golden brown and flakes when tested with a fork.

Serves 24
Per serving: calories: 160 fat: 4 g

The Palms Turkey Loaf

4	medium zucchini
3	large carrots
1½	celery stalks
2	medium onions
2	medium bell peppers
6	lb ground turkey
8	eggs
1	cup tomato puree
¼	cup tamati soy sauce
3	tbsp garlic powder
1	tbsp oregano
1	tbsp thyme
2	tbsp basil
1	tsp allspice
	arrowroot, as noted below

Wash, peel, and cut veggies finely. Grind together in a chopper. Mix ground vegetables with turkey in chopper. Mix the eggs in a blender and add to mixture. Mix the tomato puree and soy sauce and add to mixture. Grind spices in a mortar and pestle and add to mixture. Form loaves and place on a cookie sheet. Bake at 375° for 2 hours. Remove, pour off liquid, and chill liquid. Remove fat from liquid and thicken for gravy with 1 tbsp arrowroot per cup liquid.

Yield: 3 loaves
Per serving: calories: 180   fat: 9 g

The Palms Cheesecake Decalorized

3   **cups lowfat cottage cheese**
2   **egg whites**
2   **tbsp honey**
1   **tsp vanilla**
½   **tsp almond extract**
2   **tbsp lemon**

Combine all ingredients in a blender and process until creamy. Place a pan of water in the bottom of a 350° oven. Pour blender contents into a nonstick baking dish (9″ × 12″). Bake at 350° for 45 minutes, reduce oven temperature to 300°, and bake for 15 minutes longer. Chill and serve alone or with glazed fruit.

Serves 8
Per serving: calories: 80 fat: 1 g

The Pritikin Longevity Center
MIAMI BEACH, FL

Lemon Cheese Cake by Chef Tom Baggot

FILLING:

20 oz fat-free cream cheese
3 egg whites
1 tsp vanilla or cheese cake extract
1 tsp lemon zest
3 tbsp apple juice concentrate
¼ tsp nutmeg

CRUST:

½ cup nutty Rice cereal
½ cup multigrain cereal
½ tsp cinnamon
1 tbsp apple juice concentrate
¼ tsp nutmeg
¼ tsp ground cloves

Preheat oven at 350 degrees.

For filling: Blend fat-free cream cheese, vanilla, lemon zest, apple juice concentrate, and nutmeg in food processor. Set aside. Whip egg whites until they hold soft peaks. Fold into cream cheese mixture. Set aside. For crust: Pulse cereals, cinnamon, nutmeg, and cloves in food processor until coarsely chopped. Add apple juice concentrate and pulse. Form pie crust by pressing mixture into 7" pie pan. Pour cheese mixture over pie crust. Bake at 350 for 30 minutes. Refrigerate overnight.

Serves 8
Per serving: calories: 120 fat: 0 g

Rancho La Puerta

TECATE, BAJA CALIFORNIA, MEXICO

Salsa

2	tomatoes
½	onion, peeled and chopped
2	cloves garlic, cleaned
1	jalapeño chili, deseeded
1	tsp oregano, chopped
1½	cups water or vegetable stock
	salt to taste

Place all ingredients in a saucepan and add water or vegetable stock. Simmer for 15 minutes. Drain and pulse in Cuisinart until blended but still chunky. Adjust seasoning with a little salt.

Serves 3
Per serving: calories: 18 fat: 0 g

Sonoma Mission Inn & Spa

SONOMA, CA

Sauteed Prawns With Saffron Rice

5   prawns peeled and deveined
1   oz olive oil
1   oz garlic, minced
2   oz diced or crushed tomato
1   oz shallot, minced
1   oz white wine
1   oz butter
½   lemon, juiced
Mixed herbs, combine and crush in a mortar with pestle
tarragon, pinch
1   bay leaf (remove stem and central vein)
dill, pinch
salt and pepper to taste
3   oz saffron rice (recipe follows)

Sauté the prawns in olive oil over high heat until done. Remove them from the pan and keep warm. Add tomatoes, garlic, and shallots to the pan and sauté briefly. Deglaze the pan with the white wine. Return the prawns to the pan and add the butter, lemon juice, and mixed herbs. Adjust the seasoning with salt and pepper to taste. Place the rice on the plate and top rice with the prawns.

Saffron Rice

2   cups water
½   cup basmati rice
1   pinch saffron
salt and pepper to taste

Bring water to a boil. Add rice, saffron, and salt and pepper. Cover and cook approximately 20 minutes or until done.

Serves 4
Prawns and rice
Per serving: calories: 275   fat: 14 g

Turnberry Isle Resort

AVENTURA, FL

Grilled Swordfish and Tomato Herb Salsa with roasted new potatoes and steamed squash

1   lb fresh swordfish
8   small new potatoes
thyme pepper
2   small zucchini
2   yellow squash
100% vegetable oil spray
fresh cilantro
lemon slices

MARINADE:

¼   cup fresh lime juice
½   tsp ground white pepper
1¼   cups water
½   tsp cumin
¾   tsp Oregano
1   clove garlic, minced
½   tsp Salt
½   tsp sugar
2   bay leaves
1   red chili pepper, chopped, or ⅛ tsp chili pepper flakes
1   tbsp extra virgin olive oil
1   medium onion, finely diced

TOMATO HERB SALSA:

4	medium tomatoes, very ripe
1	tsp cracked coriander seed
3	tsp extra virgin olive oil
1	tbsp fresh cilantro, sliced
1	lemon, juice of
1	tbsp fresh chives, sliced
2	tbsp onion, minced
¼	tsp ground white pepper
⅛	tsp salt (optional)
4	drops Tabasco

Cut swordfish into 4-oz portions and marinate for 1–2 hours in refrigerator. While fish is marinating, prepare salsa.

First core tomatoes then drop into boiling water for 10 seconds. Remove and drop into cold water. Remove and peel skin off using a small paring knife. Remove seeds and chop finely. Place tomato and remaining salsa ingredients in a bowl and mix well. Keep at room temperature.

Brush new potatoes with extra virgin olive oil. Season with thyme and pepper. Preheat oven to 350 degrees and roast for 25–35 minutes or until done.

Cut zucchini and yellow squash into thin slices and steam for 3–5 minutes until tender crisp. Place potatoes and mixed squash on a warm plate and keep in a 150° oven while fish is cooking.

Heat grill or pan and spray with 100% vegetable oil just before adding fish. Cook total of 5–10 minutes, depending upon thickness, turning once. Swordfish should be slightly pink inside. Be careful not to overcook since swordfish can become dry.

To Serve: Heat four plates in a 150° oven. Place 4 tbsp of salsa on each. Top with 1 serving of fish and put 2 new potatoes and ½ cup of mixed squash around each. Garnish with fresh cilantro and lemon slices.

Serves 4
Per serving: calories: 300 fat: 8 g

RECIPES FROM RESTAURANTS

The "21" Club

NEW YORK, NY

Crab Cake Recipe

1   lb fresh jumbo lump crabmeat
1   sweet red pepper
1   sweet yellow pepper
¼   cup olive oil for pan frying
2   cloves fresh garlic
2   fresh jalepenno chili peppers
¼   cup chopped cilantro leaves
3   tbsp mayonnaise
2   tbsp bread crumbs, reserve ½ cup additional bread crumbs for coating
2   tbsp OLD BAY brand seasoning powder
salt and fresh ground pepper to taste

Carefully clean the crabmeat of all shell fragments but do not crumble the lumps of crab. Cut the sweet peppers in half and remove the seeds. Cut the peppers into a small dice, sauté in 1 tsp of olive oil and set them aside. Chop the fresh garlic cloves into a fine dice or crush in a garlic press. Clean the jalepenno peppers of their seeds and dice these finely. Mix the crabmeat with sweet peppers, garlic, jalepenno, chopped cilantro leaves and mayonnaise. Add bread-crumbs, seasoning powder, salt, and pepper, and refrigerate for 20 minutes before continuing.

Using an ice cream scoop, form eight equal-sized balls, and using the palm of your hand, pat them into disc shapes similar to a hockey puck. This is the basic form of the crab cake.

Sprinkle the reserve bread crumbs onto your work area and press the cakes into them one at a time to coat evenly on all sides.

When the cakes are completed, heat the remaining olive oil in a sauté pan until just before it begins to smoke. Add the crab cakes carefully but do not crowd the pan. Cook them in two batches if necessary.

When they are well browned on both sides, remove from the pan and keep them warm. This cooking process does not take a long time to complete and should not be done too far in advance.

When you are ready to serve the crab cakes, a small salad can be served on the same plate along with some mayonnaise flavored with ground chili paste, mustard, and horseradish or cocktail sauce.

Serves 8
Per serving: calories: 190   fat: 12 g

Mr. Chow

KYOTO, LONDON, NEW YORK,

BEVERLY HILLS

Chicken Joanna

2	chicken breast
1	tsp salt
½	tsp. white pepper
½	tsp. sesame oil
1	cup flour
2	eggs
3	tbsp. vegetable oil
2	cloves garlic
1	scallion
⅓	cup chicken broth
1	tsp. vinegar
2	pieces cilantro

Slice each chicken breast into two pieces. Add a little salt, white pepper powder, and a few drops of sesame oil and marinate for a minute. Then coat with flour, dip in eggs, and remove for pan frying.

Heat vegetable oil in wok and cook chicken until golden brown on both sides. Add garlic, chopped scallion, rest of salt, and chicken broth. Cook for two more minutes, add vinegar and rest of sesame oil and remove cooked chicken.

Serve by covering with remaining juices from pan and sprinkle with cilantro.

Serves 8
Per serving: calories: 190 fat: 12 g

Cafe' Pierre

NEW YORK, NY

Grilled Snapper, Baby Vegetables, and Aromatic Bouillon

SNAPPER

6 fillets scaled red snapper (6 oz each)
salt and pepper to taste
3 tbsp olive oil

AROMATIC BOUILLON

6 cups fresh fish fumet
5 tbsp extra virgin olive oil
2 kaffir leaves
1 tbsp chopped fresh thyme
1 tbsp chopped fresh rosemary
1 tbsp chopped fresh opal basil
1 tbsp chopped fennel hair
1 tbsp chopped fresh-picked coriander
2 cloves thinly sliced garlic
2 stocks fennel
3 tbsp small brunoise red peppers, minced
3 tbsp small brunoise yellow peppers, minced
salt and white pepper to taste
Baby vegetables
6 cups assorted steamed baby vegetables, such
   as broccoli, carrots, string beans, squash

Preheat extremely clean grill on the burner. Season the snapper on both sides with salt and pepper. Lightly brush the snapper with a bit of olive oil on both sides. When grill is very hot, mark the snapper right and left side to produce even squares on the skin side. Set aside.

In a large creuset, pour the cold fish fumet and add all other ingredients. Season lightly with salt and pepper and stir to mix the ingredients.

To serve, one fillet in each plate, surround approximately ½ cup of baby vegetables, ladle stock around fillet. (Make sure stock does not cover the fish.)

Serves 6
Per serving: calories: 300 fat: 13 g

Cafe Roma

BEVERLY HILLS, CA

White Fish alla Livornese

2   **white fish fillets, lightly floured**
3   **tbsp extra virgin olive oil**
salt
1   **clove garlic**
½   **tbsp chopped parsley**
1   **cup fresh crushed tomatoes**
2   **oz dry white wine**
½   **cup pitted black olives**
½   **tbsp capers**

Dredge the fillets in flour. Heat the oil in a large frying pan and brown the fillets over fairly high heat. Season with salt. Add the garlic, parsley, and fresh tomatoes; cook down. Pour the wine, add the olives and capers, and cook over moderate heat for 3 minutes, turning the fillets so that they are well basted with the sauce.

Turn out onto a heated platter and serve immediately with a side of steamed spinach.

Serves 2
Per serving: calories: 475   fat: 29 g

Le Dôme

BEVERLY HILLS, CA

Tartar of Oysters and Two Caviars

18	fresh Pacific oysters
2	shallots
2	tbsp capers
2	tbsp fresh lemon juice
2	tbsp sour cream

salt and pepper

3	oz golden caviar
2	oz sturgeon caviar (American or Russian)

Soak oysters, reserving shell and juice. Chop shallots, capers, and parsley. Cut oysters in small pieces and mix everything with lemon juice, sour cream, a small amount of oyster juice, salt, and pepper.

Fill each shell with the oyster tartar, line the outer rim with golden caviar, and top it with a dab of American or Russian (Sevruga) caviar in the center.

Serves 6
Per serving: calories: 255 fat: 10 g

The Grill

BEVERLY HILLS, CA

Chicken Burger

2   lbs chicken leg and thigh meat (boneless and skinless)
1   lb chicken breast (boneless and skinless)
½   cup "mango" apple chutney
1   tsp white pepper

With a ³⁄₁₆″ blade, grind all chicken meat and blend together with the other ingredients. Form into 8-oz patties and cook for 6–8 minutes, on open skillet. Cover burger while cooking and turning pattie over 2–3 times.

Serves 6
Per serving: calories: 300   fat: 13 g

Beverly Hills Hotel

BEVERLY HILLS, CA

McCarthy Salad

2	cups Bibb lettuce, chopped
1.5	oz cooked chicken breast
2	oz fresh tomato
1	strip bacon, cooked crisp
1.5	oz hard-boiled egg
2	oz beets
1	oz cheddar cheese, shredded

Arrange bed of lettuce on plate. Finely dice chicken, tomato, cooked bacon, egg, and beets. Arrange attractively on the lettuce. Top with shredded cheese. Serve with flavored vinegar or other light dressing.

Servings: 1
Per Serving: Calories: 275 Fat 15 g

Delphi Greek Cuisine
LOS ANGELES, CA
Potato Salad El Greco

1   **head romaine lettuce**
1   **tomato**
1   **cucumber**
3   **boiled potatoes**
a few capers
½   **bunch scallions**

Cut lettuce into small pieces and wash. After washing, drain. Place in strainer. Cut tomato into 8 wedges. Slice cucumber. Place cucumber pieces around plate. Put lettuce in the center of plate. Cut potatoes in small pieces mixed with capers and chopped scallions and vinaigrette dressing and place them on top of lettuce. Garnish the salad with tomato wedges.

Serves 3–4
Per serving: calories: 200 fat: .5 g (without dressing)

The Bistro Garden
STUDIO CITY, CA
Chocolate Soufflé

12	egg yolks
26	oz sugar
1	dash vanilla
13	oz flour
1	quart milk
4	squares of unsweetened chocolate
20	egg whites

dash of salt
butter and sugar to coat Soufflé forms

Combine egg yolks with 12oz sugar and vanilla. Mix well. Add flour and stir until it forms a smooth paste. Bring the milk to a boil in a pot and add the paste-like mixture to the milk; allow this to boil for 2–3 minutes before stirring (when it is time to stir, do so with a whisk). Remove and clean the whisk, and using a wooden spatula, stir until the paste removes itself from the sides of the pot.

Melt the chocolate. Put the paste mixture into a pastry mixer for approximately 15–20 minutes; then add the melted chocolate and mix well. Place this in a large mixing bowl and allow to cool.

Place the egg whites in a mixing bowl with a dash of salt and whip until they begin to form stiff, meringue-like peaks, then add remaining sugar 14 oz for the meringue. Add ⅓ of the whites to the cooled paste, mixing with a rubber spatula. Continue, using three steps to fold in all the whites. Use 6-oz soufflé forms, coated on the inside with butter and sugar. Cook for 15–18 minutes at 375°.

Serves 12–16
Per serving: calories: 460 fat: 11 g

Le Cirque 2000

NEW YORK, NY

Strawberry Terrine

18   **oz nonfat yogurt**
18   **oz fresh strawberries**
7   **oz sugar**
4   **oz corn syrup**
4   **oz water**
7   **oz egg whites**
juice of 1 lemon
6   **gelatin sheets**
8   **mango slices**
8   **thin slices of white bread**

Whip non-fat yogurt and refrigerate. Puree fresh strawberries and refrigerate. Combine sugar, corn syrup, and water. Boil and bring to soft ball stage.

While boiling the above, lightly whip egg whites with the juice of one lemon into mixture.

Add six gelatin sheets, softened in cold water. Carefully fold the yogurt into the strawberries into the boiled sugar.

Line a terrine with a mango slice. Fill to ¼ from the top with the strawberry mixture. Close with thin slices of white bread soaked with strawberry puree. Let harden in refrigerator for about 1 hour. Unfold and serve.

Serves 8
Per serving: calories: 255   fat: 1 g

Spago

BEVERLY HILLS, CA

Stir-Fried Vegetables

1   tbsp peanut oil
½   lb Chinese snow peas, cut into 1-in chunks
2   oz oyster mushrooms, whole or cut in half, depending upon size
2   oz shiitake mushrooms, whole or cut in half, stems removed (stems can be added to stocks for flavor)
2   oz each red and yellow bell pepper strips, cut into 1-in chunks
½   large Japanese eggplant, cut into 6 or 7 slices
¼   medium bok choy, cut into 1-in chunks
6   broccoli florets
5   young asparagus, cut into 1½- to 2-in lengths
⅓   cup chicken stock, heated
1   tbsp soy sauce
salt
freshly ground pepper

The combination of the oil, stock, and soy sauce produces a glaze for the vegetables. When cooked, the vegetables should be shiny and crispy with no stock remaining in the pan.

In a wok or large skillet, heat the oil. Over high heat, stir-fry all the vegetables, coating them with the oil. Pour in the stock and the soy sauce and stir until al dente, about 2 minutes longer. Season with salt and pepper to taste, keeping in mind that the soy sauce is salty. Serve immediately.

Serves 2–4
Per serving: calories: 110   fat: 5 g

RECIPES OF THE CELEBRITIES

Ivana Trump's Chicken Paprika

1	frying chicken, about 2½ lbs
½	cup + 2 tbsp flour
½	tsp salt
½	tsp white pepper
2	tbsp + 1 tsp sweet Hungarian paprika
1½	tbsp butter
1½	tbsp vegetable oil
1	cup yellow onion, finely chopped
2	cups well-seasoned chicken stock
1	cup cultured sour cream

Disjoint the chicken. Dust chicken pieces with ½ cup flour seasoned with salt, white pepper, and 1 tsp sweet Hungarian paprika.

Melt butter and vegetable oil in a heavy saucepan. Sauté chicken in heated butter and oil until browned and remove from the pan.

Add yellow onion and 2 tbsp sweet Hungarian paprika to the pan.

When onions are translucent, return chicken to pan and add chicken stock. Simmer covered until tender, about 1 hour.

Stir 2 tbsp flour into the cultured sour cream. Add slowly into pot and simmer until thickened and smooth. Do not boil or sour cream could separate.

Serve with noodles or rice.

Serves 4
Per serving: calories: 425 fat: 26 g

Robert Evans's Lemon Soufflé

12 egg whites
10 egg yolks
⅔ cup sugar
½ cup lemon juice, freshly squeezed
butter to coat pan

Separate egg whites and whip until peaked. Whip egg yolks with ⅔ cup sugar. Whip lemon juice into sugar and yolk mixture. Whip egg whites again briefly. Fold egg yolks with egg whites. Pour into soufflé dish which has already been buttered.

Cook in pre heated oven at 275° for 30 minutes.

Serves 6
Per serving: calories: 170 fat: 6.5 g

Beverly D'Angelo's Zucchini Curry Soup

1½	**lb zucchini**
2	**bunches scallion shallots**
	(*ratio of zucchini to shallots: 2–1 to 3–2*)
2	**leeks chop, cleaned and chopped**
2	**cups chicken broth, canned**
½	**tsp curry powder**
½	**tsp cumin**

Steam zucchini, scallions, and leeks. Puree with remaining ingredients. Cook for 10 minutes. Serve hot or cold.

Serves 2
Per cup: calories: 60 fat: .5 g

Beverly Johnson's Roast Salmon
with Vine Ripe Tomato-Pepper Salsa, Polenta, and Sugar Snap Peas

POLENTA

3½	cups boiling water
1½	tsp kosher salt
1	cup cornmeal
1	tbsp cornmeal for dusting

SALMON AND MARINADE

6	5–6 oz Norwegian salmon fillets
4	oz orange juice
2	oz lemon juice
2	oz soy sauce

SALSA

1	roasted red pepper, medium dice
1	roasted yellow pepper, medium dice
1	roasted Peblano pepper, medium dice
3	medium vine-ripened tomatoes, cut into medium dice
1	stalk celery, from the heart, small dice
1	small red onion, minced
½	avocado, medium dice
2	cloves minced garlic
⅛	tsp salt
¼	tsp black pepper
¼	tsp chili powder
¼	tsp cumin
1½	limes, juiced
pinch	cayenne pepper
2	tbsp chopped parsley
4	tbsp chopped fresh cilantro
¼	cup balsamic vinegar
2	lb sugar snap peas

Bring water and salt to a boil and slowly whisk in the cornmeal. Cover and simmer over a low flame for fifteen minutes. Pour the polenta into a shallow, square baking pan and refrigerate. Then, cooled sufficiently, cut into three six-inch squares, ½ inch thick and then into triangles. Cover with a wet towel and refrigerate.

For the salsa, roast the peppers over an open flame until charred, transfer to a plate, and let cool. Up to this point the recipe can be prepared one day ahead.

Combine the salsa ingredients in a non reactive, stainless steel bowl. Let stand 1–2 hours to allow flavors to bloom. When ready to serve, place salmon in the marinade for a half-hour, preheat the oven to 375,° and bring two quarts of water to a boil. After a half-hour, remove the salmon from the marinade, place onto a baking sheet, and bake about 7–10 minutes or until medium pink. Sprinkle polenta squares with a little cornmeal and place on another tray: bake 5–6 minutes. Blanch the snap peas in the boiling water. To serve, place salsa in the bottom of six shallow bowls, arrange snap peas around with two polenta squares per serving and the salmon steak in the middle.

Serves 6
Per serving: calories: 525 fat: 16 g

Joan Rivers's Turkey Burgers

1   lb ground white turkey meat
2   oz low-fat mozzarella cheese, coarsely shredded
8   tbsp bottled roasted garlic salsa
4   tbsp nonfat plain yogurt
salt and pepper to taste
4   hamburger buns

Combine turkey, cheese, 4 tbsp salsa, and salt and pepper and shape into four patties. Combine 4 tbsp salsa and yogurt (to be used as sauce). Heat a non stick pan until it is medium-hot. Spray with Pam and sauté patties until they are browned and cooked through (about 5–7 minutes. Serve on buns with yogurt sauce and sliced tomatoes.

Serves 4
Per serving: calories: 380   fat: 16.5 g

Alan Thicke's Sister's Livers

12	oz chicken livers
3	tbsp soy sauce
1–2	cloves pressed garlic
½	tsp chopped fresh ginger
2	sliced green onions
1	tsp liquid artificial sweetener

Combine all ingredients. Marinate for 1–2 hours. Then broil, turning until livers are slightly pink inside. Serve with brown rice and salad.

Serves 2
Per serving: calories: 280 fat: 9 g

Paul Newman's P. Loquesort's Chicken Creole

1 medium onion, chopped
1 green pepper, chopped
1 tbsp vegetable oil
2 cups diced, cooked chicken
1 cup cooked rice
2 cups Newman's Own spaghetti sauce (naturally!)
dash of ground nutmeg

Sauté onion and pepper in oil until limp. Add chicken, rice, spaghetti sauce, and nutmeg. Simmer, covered, over low heat for 45 minutes or bake at 350° for 45 minutes.

Serves 4
Per serving: calories: 340 fat: 11 g

Jill St. John's Lemon Grass Sea Bass

4   **8-oz Chilean sea bass fillets**
2   **bulbs lemon grass thinly sliced**
2   **tbsp Chinese rice wine vinegar**
1   **tsp unflavored sesame oil**
1   **tsp fresh lemon juice**
dash of soy sauce
1   **slice peeled ginger**

Fill a large frying pan halfway with water and invert a pie pan in the center. Cover the frying pan with a tight-fitting lid and bring the water to a boil. Place all of the ingredients in a deep 9-inch plate. Turn the fish once or twice to be sure that both sides are covered with the lemon grass mixture. Place the plate on top of the inverted pie plate. Recover pan, lower heat, and allow to steam for about 10 minutes. Serve on heated plates and spoon some of the liquid over the fish.

Serves 4
Per serving: calories: 275   fat: 9.5 g

Loni Anderson's Seafood Salad

1	box macaroni shells
2	small cans shrimp
2	cans (or fresh) fancy crab meat
2	cans low-sodium tuna in water
2	cup celery, chopped
½	cup chopped scallion
	lowfat mayonnaise to taste
	salt and pepper to taste

Cook shells until al dente and let cool. Combine with other ingredients and serve.

Serves 4
Per serving: calories: 410 fat: 5 g

Sandra Di Portanova's Sunset Shrimp Surrealist

¼   **cup finely chopped onion**
1   **clove garlic, minced**
1½   **tsp chili powder**
1½   **tsp paprika**
1   **cup lemon or lime juice**
2   **tbsp Worcestershire sauce**
3   **dashes hot red-pepper sauce**
12   **jumbo shrimp, shelled and deveined, heads and tails intact**
Butter Buds, melted

In a bowl, combine the onion, garlic, chili powder, paprika, lemon or lime juice, Worcestershire, and hot pepper sauce. Blend well. Add the shrimp, cover, and marinate them overnight in the refrigerator.

To cook, arrange the shrimp on skewers and barbecue them, basting with the melted Butter Buds until they are done. Serve the shrimp on the skewers at sunset with chilled dry white wine or champagne.

Serves 2
Per serving: calories: 130   fat: 4 g

LeRoy Neiman's Linguine with Spinach, Pine Nuts, and Parmesan Cheese

1   lb linguine
½   cup olive oil
4   oz fresh spinach, trimmed
1   cup freshly grated Parmesan cheese
Salt and pepper to taste
½   cup pine nuts, toasted

Cook linguine in large pot of boiling salted water until just tender but still firm to bite, stirring occasionally.

Meanwhile, heat oil in heavy, large skillet over medium heat. Add trimmed spinach that has been cut in approx. 1-in strips and stir until just wilted, about 30 seconds. Remove from heat.

Drain pasta and return to pot. Add spinach and toss well. Add 1 cup Parmesan and salt and pepper to taste; toss well. Transfer to bowl. Sprinkle with pine nuts. Serve immediately, passing additional Parmesan separately.

Serves 4
Per serving: calories: 560   fat: 42 g

Fabio's Pasta Salad Primavera

1	tbsp extra virgin olive oil
1	tbsp balsamic vinegar
2	cloves garlic, minced
½	tsp Dijon style mustard
½	tsp Italian seasoning blend dash of salt and pepper
2	tbsp green onion, thinly sliced
2	tsp sugar substitute
1½	oz rotelli pasta
¼	cup each red and green pepper, finely chopped
¼	cup each raw carrots and celery, finely chopped
½	cup blanched broccoli chopped

In a small, non aluminum bowl, whisk together oil, vinegar, garlic, mustard, and seasonings. Cook pasta until tender, approx. 7 minutes. Drain. Toss hot pasta in dressing until thoroughly coated. Add remaining ingredients and chill two hours.

Serves 1
Per serving: calories: 340 fat: 15 g

Traci Bingham's Couscous Tabboleh with Shrimp

1	red, yellow, and green bell pepper
1½	cups couscous
1¼	cups boiling water
½	tsp sea salt
4	tomatoes peeled, seeded, and diced
1	bunch scallions, chopped
½	cup chopped fresh parsley
¼	cup chopped fresh mint leaves
¼	cup fresh lemon juice
2	tbsp olive oil
freshly ground black pepper	
12	medium shrimp, peeled and deveined

Roast bell peppers under broiler until evenly charred. Transfer peppers to a paper bag and let steam for 10 minutes. Put couscous in a large bowl and stir in boiling water. Cover and let sit for 10–15 minutes, fluffing occasionally with fork. Stir peppers, tomatoes, scallions, parsley, mint leaves, lemon juice, olive oil, and black pepper into couscous. Let mixture sit for 20 minutes at room temperature to mingle flavors. Grill shrimp under broiler for 2 minutes or until pink. Arrange shrimp over couscous mixture, serve immediately.

Serves 4
Per serving: calories: 200 fat: 7 g

Suzanne Pleshette's Salmon Mousse Recipe

1	envelope unflavored gelatin
2	tbsp lemon juice
1	small slice onion
½	cup boiling water
½	cup mayonnaise
¼	tsp paprika
1	tsp dry dill
8	1-lb can salmon, drained
1	cup heavy cream

Put gelatin in blender, add lemon juice, onion, and water. Blend at high speed for 40 seconds. Add mayonnaise, dill, paprika, and salmon. Blend at high speed. Add cream ⅓ at a time, blending at each addition. Blend 30 seconds more, pour into 4 cup mold and chill.

I use a fish mold. When I remove it, I place it on a platter and I decorate it with cucumbers, pimientos, and capers. I form gills and eyes, and cover the body with overlapping cucumber slices to form scales. Scallions can make a pretty tail, but use your own imagination.

I serve this as an appetizer in the living room before we move to the table for dinner. If I'm flush, I serve caviar and diced onions to garnish along with thinly sliced pumpernickel bread to slather it on. For dieters, I encourage them to run up and down the fourteen floors from our apartment to the lobby, before going to the entrée.

Serves 4
Per serving: calories: 380 fat: 16.5 g

George Hamilton's Healthy Lunch Pita Sandwich

2   cup cooked chopped chicken breast
1   cup chopped celery
2   tbsp golden raisins
2   tbsp chopped green onions
⅓   cup low-fat mayonnaise
1   tbsp lemon juice
½   tsp curry powder
1   cup fresh spinach leaves, washed
1   red apple, sliced
2   large whole-wheat pita pockets, halved

In a medium bowl, combine chicken, celery, raisins, and green onions. In another bowl, combine mayonnaise, lemon juice, and curry powder and mix well. Pour dressing over chicken mixture and mix well. Arrange one quarter of the spinach leaves and one quarter of the apple slices in each pocket. Spoon one quarter of chicken salad mixture into each pocket.

Makes 4 sandwiches
Per serving: calories: 285   fat: 5.5 g

Goldie Hawn's Sautéed Shrimp

2   lbs raw shrimp, shelled
¼   cup olive oil
2   tbsp low-cal margarine
1   tsp salt
dash of pepper
2   cloves garlic, minced
3   tbsp parsley, minced
2   tbsp scallion, chipped
½   cup tomatoes, chopped
½   cup mushrooms, sliced
1   tbsp lemon juice
¼   cup white wine

Thoroughly clean shrimp and drain excess water.

Heat oil and low-cal margarine in a large skillet. Add shrimp to oil mixture and sauté over low heat for 4 minutes. Do not overcook. Add salt, pepper, and garlic and cook an additional 2 minutes.

Sprinkle remaining ingredients over shrimp mixture and simmer until hot.

Serves 6
Per serving: calories: 275   fat: 13 g

Liza Minnelli's Salad de Provence

2	cup cooked yellow corn
1	pink grapefruit, cut into bite-size pieces
1	cup hearts of palm
¼	cup thinly sliced fresh mushrooms
2	tbsp vinaigrette dressing made with safflower oil

Mix together and serve.

Serves 2
Per serving: calories: 240 fat: 7 g

Barbara Rush's Key Lime Pie

1   can (15 oz) sweetened condensed milk
⅓   cup fresh lime juice
1   tbsp grated lime rind
¼   tsp salt
1   baked graham cracker crust
whipped cream (optional)

Combine condensed milk, lime juice, grated rind, and salt.

No need to cook! Pour into baked pie shell and chill at least 3 hours.

Top with whipped cream if desired.

Serves 6
Per serving: calories: 475   fat: 20 g

Robert Stack's Curried Cream Spinach

1   package frozen, chopped spinach
½   can Aunt Penny's White Sauce or make
**   your own from scratch**
½   tsp Lea & Perrins Worcestershire Sauce
⅛   tsp curry powder

Prepare spinach in sauce pan. Pour off water and add the remaining ingredients.

Serves 2–3
Per serving: calories: 165   fat: 5 g

Don Rickles's Glazed Turkey Steaks

2   **tbsp orange marmalade**
1   **tbsp lemon or lime juice**
2   **tbsp soy sauce**
1   **clove garlic, minced**
¼   **tsp curry powder**
4   **4-oz turkey breasts tenderloin steaks**

In a small bowl, stir together marmalade, lemon or lime juice, soy sauce, garlic, and curry powder. Brush some of the glaze over both sides of turkey steaks. Grill turkey on an uncovered grill directly over medium coals for 6 minutes. Turn and brush with glaze. Grill 6–9 minutes more or until turkey is tender and no longer pink.

Serves 4
Per serving: calories: 170   fat: 4 g

Neil Sedaka's Voodoo Chicken

1   chicken (2½–3 lbs), cut into serving pieces
½   cup white vinegar
2   tbsp soy sauce
1   large onion, sliced
4   cloves garlic, peeled but left whole
½   tsp black pepper
4   tbsp Dijon mustard
6   tbsp ketchup
2   tbsp milk

Marinate chicken for several hours in combined vinegar, soy sauce, onion, garlic, and pepper. Drain, reserving liquid.

Combine mustard with 4 tbsp of ketchup and dip each piece of chicken into this mixture, coating well.

Bake chicken, skin side down, at 350°, for 30 minutes. Turn pieces and pour the remaining ketchup, mixed with the milk and reserved marinade, over the chicken. Bake an additional 45 minutes.

Serve with white rice.

Serves 4
Per serving: calories: 235   fat: 5 g

CHAPTER EIGHT

All Stressed Up and Nowhere to Go

"I keep trying to lose weight, but it keeps finding me."

George Burns and me at his 98th Birthday Bash.

With Frank Sinatra in Palm Springs.

S tress. The creepy, intense, tiger-by-the tail psychosocial pressure which bugs us all. From midwest farmhouse to big-city stock exchange, there is no escaping some form of it in our daily lives. To many, the stress of day-to-day living is a vital, invigorating element which adds excitement to what otherwise would be a ho-hum existence. To others, however, the pressure is overwhelming. The emotional strings are twisted tighter and tighter. And in an effort to seek solace, we turn to food.

In a study by the American Psychological Association, it was revealed that food was the single most common relief for stress used by adults in this country. This shouldn't come as a surprise to any of us. Unfortunately, eating doesn't solve the problem; it simply compounds it. When stress eating gets out of hand, we simply add obesity to our growing list of stresses.

The key to handling stress is to understand it. What amounts to stress for one person means little or nothing to another. Identifying what causes stress in your life, and taking steps to reduce or control it, is the secret. This does not mean that you should immediately begin taking this week's most popular tranquilizer, or sign up with the nearest meditation ashram. Everyone, regardless of the intensity of stress in their lives, can take simple logical steps to *control* it. Without control, you are living in a house built on quicksand which could, and most likely will, come tumbling down around you.

I have discovered the easiest and most effective ways to handle stress in my own life. As a businesswoman, Star Dieter, and celebrity hostess, my schedule is as intense as anyone's. These ten steps have never failed to bring me through in a collected, organized, and reasonably stress-free manner. The next time you hang up the phone and want to reach for a cookie, try these instead.

Step 1. Schedule your meals.

It's not enough to pay attention to *what* you eat; it is important to know *when* you are eating as well. One of the problems that "food addicts" have is that they have no concept of how many times during a day they actually consume food. By scheduling your meals and sticking to the schedule, you take control of one more aspect of your life.

Step 2. Exercise.

Exercising daily not only improves your metabolism and overall health; it reduces stress as well. The endorphin levels in your blood rise when you exercise regularly. Endorphins are your body's natural sedative. Take advantage of what nature has to offer. Suzanne Pleshette advises that if you have a dog, take your dog with you for those nice long walks. It makes exercising much more fun and animals are known to reduce stress.

Step 3. Maintain a uniform sleep pattern.

Regardless of how many hours you sleep, it is most important that you maintain a consistent sleep pattern. For some people this means 8 hours a night. Everybody's system is different. Madame Marcos slept 1 hour a night and took two naps during the day. Albert Einstein reportedly never slept for more than 3 hours at a time. He just took catnaps during the day. I like to get about 4 to 6 hours of sleep.

The body needs rest to repair and replenish itself. If you have trouble falling asleep, begin by developing a pattern in which you repeat the same pre-bed routine each night. Mine is wash, pamper, read, watch TV, doze. You'll be surprised at how quickly your body learns that the routine means sleep.

I take a nap every day of my life. I get some of my most restful sleep during that nap time. I had to train myself to take a nap. I found that I was getting overly tired and irritable in the late afternoon. I would come home from the office, put on my nightgown, turn off the telephone, and get in bed and close my eyes. It took several attempts before I actually fell asleep. When I did, I found that it relieved tension and anxiety. Even if you can't fall asleep, it's very restful just to lie down and close your eyes anywhere from 10 minutes to an hour. You may find that you sleep better at night if you nap during the day.

Naps are extremely helpful when traveling. Taking little catnaps while flying helps to prevent jet lag. Whenever I travel (as so many others do), I always take a nap between five and seven in the evening. This helps me readjust my sleeping habits to the time of the city or country that I am in. I feel awake and refreshed for several hours. Remember, good sleeping habits are the best defense against stress.

Step 4. Cut Out Coffee; Give Up the Cola.

In fact, remove caffeine from your diet as much as possible. If you simply must have the morning cup to get going, limit it to that one cup—then get going. Never forget that caffeine is addictive and your body will require increasing amounts. Break the cycle if you can, or better yet, don't start it.

Step 5. Share Yourself with Others.

Give your friends and family attention and affection. By steering your concentration away from yourself, you not only help others, but defuse your own stress in the process. If you happen to live alone, lavish your affection on a pet. Even a house plant will do. Give of yourself and you'll reap the benefits many times over.

Step 6. Rely on Family Members or Trusted Friends for Emotional Support.

In our transient society, it has become harder and harder to form lasting relationships. Yet no one can make it through life alone. Even if they're not close by, and even if it's not often, an occasional visit or a heart-to-heart on the phone with a family member can give you a sense of belonging and does wonders to relieve anxiety. It relieves the stress of feeling that we're alone in the world. If no family members exist, or if they are at such a distance that communication is impossible on a continuing basis, form a family of friends you can rely on. Sharing your thoughts is not a burden on others. It's a give-and-take proposition which will help them as much as it does you.

Step 7. Schedule some quiet time for yourself.

Just as you must spend some time with others, so you must spend some time alone. Even if you have two kids, a dog, and a plumber in the kitchen, find some quiet time for yourself. Each of us deserves a small period of solitude every day. It's remarkably healing. This is especially important if you live with a house full of people. Find a room, close the door, and leave the world behind for ten minutes or as long as you need. Once again, you must schedule this downtime. If you consider it optional or leave it to chance, it will never happen. Treat it like an appointment with your favorite person—you. There is nothing more important you will do during the day. Do something that you've always wanted to do. Take up painting or join a drawing class. Pottery or sculpting is a wonderful way of working with your hands and relieving anxiety. Take a photography course. I found that nothing is more fun than the collection of sunset pictures that I have accumulated over the years. It has given me great pleasure and hours of relaxation.

Step 8. Join a group.

It doesn't really matter what the group is—a church, synagogue, club, or organization. The important thing is to get out and participate in life. Bowl, join a bridge club, volunteer at a hospital, clean up community graffiti, feed the homeless, become a Big Brother, join a charity. There is nothing more rewarding than working with under-privileged children. It takes your mind off yourself. You know the old expression, "I cried because I had no shoes till I saw the man who had no feet." Your worries will seem much smaller when you realize how much luckier you are than most people in the world. The time you spend with others is time you spend on yourself. Humans are social beings; we were never intended to live alone. It's too easy to become isolated these days. Don't let it happen to you. Schedule your activities so that it becomes part of your regular routine.

Step 9. Pay attention to your appearance.

Not all of us look like movie stars, but we can all make an effort to look our best. The more effort you make to look good, the better you will feel about yourself, and the less likely you will go off your diet. It's remarkable what simple grooming can do to raise our self-esteem. I never leave the house unless well groomed. It's a wonderful feeling to know that if the unexpected happens (meeting a friend from college, an ex-lover, a future lover, an unexpected surprise party), you'll never be embarrassed by the way you look. Looking good is feeling good.

Step 10. Learn to love yourself.

At the end of each day, reflect on the good things that have happened to you. Pat yourself on the back when you do something well; congratulate yourself for simply surviving another day. Not everybody does. Go dancing and have fun. The fact that you have reached your daily goals is a positive step. Give yourself a little applause. You deserve it. You're a winner. Don't be afraid to live out your dreams.

You will notice that there are three underlying themes in the ten steps I've recommended. First: Schedule your time. The person who is in control of his own destiny is a person who has reduced his stress. Second: Connect with others. Too much time alone can make life's challenges seem overwhelming. Third: Be good to yourself. Don't punish yourself. If you're not good to yourself, chances are nobody else will be. In today's society, everyone seems to want a piece of your time or energy. Just as it is important to give *of* yourself, it's equally important to give *to* yourself. Take time out to take care of yourself. There are many wonderful ways to do so.

The luxury I love best is a *massage and/or a facial*. To have the tense muscles of my neck and back relaxed through precise manipulation does more than relieve stress. It actually releases toxins in the muscle tissues at the same time. If a professional massage is a financial impossibility, an amateur can be a close second. Get your husband, wife, lover, or friend to give you a back rub. It's the commitment to doing something for yourself that's important.

Another way to relax and relieve pent-up tension is through *aromatherapy*. With this technique, fragrant oils are massaged into the body at points determined by the ancient practice of accupressure. Depending on the fragrant oil you select, you will find yourself stimulated, inspired, mellowed, or soothed. This technique does require a professional. Unless you're married to an accupunturist, you can't get this kind of treatment from an amateur.

Another technique is *shiatsu*. In Japanese, *shiatsu* means "finger" *(shi)* "pressure" *(atsu)*. The skilled shiatsu technician uses his fingers against accupressure points to unblock energy channels and release toxins from the system. There is no actual muscle massage involved in shiatsu, but the end result is much the same. You will leave a shiatsu session feeling relaxed and refreshed.

A final massage application is *reflexology*. With this technique, a specific part of the body—typically the foot or the hand—is analyzed for tenderness, tightness, or actual pain. The skilled reflexologist is then able to pinpoint corresponding weakness or tightness in the body as a whole. As the painful area of the foot or hand is massaged, the corresponding distressed area of the body is soothed. Don't ask me how rubbing your feet helps your head, but it does. It also helps stiff necks, bad backs, and strained muscles in many people. A welcome by-product of the technique is the relief of tension.

Many people also benefit from meditation and yoga in relieving stress and diminishing anxiety. Both yoga and meditation are time-honored methods of relaxing and finding inner strength. Either may work for you.

As for me, I prefer activity as a way to relieve tension. After an especially stressful day, the worst thing for me is to climb into bed and pull the covers over my head. Instead, I get out and have fun. I put on my best dress, call a friend, and go dancing. I defy anyone to spend several hours on the dance floor with an attractive dance partner and feel tense at the end of evening. If you can't find a partner to go out with, try something active on your own. Put on a video and dance in your own living room. You'll feel better and speed up your metabolism in the process.

All of this brings me back to the basic premise: Whatever you do when you feel stressed, *don't eat*. Despite the natural instinct to put food in your mouth at the first sign of tension, frustration, or disappointment, stress eating is a self-defeating mechanism. First of all, a full stomach doesn't help. It doesn't relieve the tension, and it certainly does nothing to treat the cause of the problem. Second, the weight you will gain from stress-induced eating will only create more stress, setting up a vicious cycle. If you must put something in your mouth when you're tense, make a delicious cup of chamomile tea and take a few minutes to sip it quietly. By the time you reach the bottom of the cup, you will be thinking more calmly and clearly.

DYING TO BE THIN

Before I finish, I want to make something very clear. All of us suffer from occasional anxiety and stress. And all of us eat from stress sometimes. But for some people, the problem is much more serious. Some of us develop serious psychological disorders that influence how we relate to food and to our bodies. Sadly, too many people are dying to be thin. Eating disorders are growing by epidemic proportions in this decade. One such disorder is bulimia. The bulimia sufferer goes on secret, episodic food binges, consuming up to 50,000 calories in a single day, and then forces herself to throw up. The anorexic, on the other hand, is so terrified of losing control of her food intake that she won't eat at all. Her body image becomes severely distorted. No matter how thin she gets, she sees a fat person in the mirror. Over half of all anorexics have bouts of bulimia as well. Over 95 percent of these groups consist of middle-or upper-class white women. But they're not the only ones. Many men have the same problem. Anorexics want to look like Barbie and Ken but they end up looking like skeletons.

Another debilitating eating disorder is compulsive overeating. This group is composed equally of men and women who substitute food for emotional involvement. Typically, the compulsive overeater was neglected or abused as a child and uses food to soothe the pain. Compulsive eaters don't just binge every now and then; unable to control their food intake, they will eat huge amounts until they are sick.

The final disorder I'm concerned about is exercise addiction. The exercise addict works out constantly, yet never feels it is enough. The exercise addict, like the anorexic, has a distorted body image which makes her believe her body is never good enough. Almost exclusively a female complex, this newly recognized disease is a response to cultural pressure to have the so-called "perfect body" that everyone wants and no one ever achieves.

All four disorders share a common tragedy: They all do enormous damage to the body and spirit. The anorexic suffers permanent hormonal damage, muscle cramps, constipation, a decreased heart rate, and in some cases, death from cardiac arrest. The bulimic experiences erosion of dental enamel, burns on the inside of the mouth and the esophagus, and kidney failure. The compulsive overeater is prone to heart attacks, diabetes, and liver failure. And the exercise addict experiences joint and cartilage damage, bone fractures, and broken blood vessels that steadily debilitate the body.

If you recognize any of these symptoms in yourself, you are beyond the reach of simple stress reduction techniques. You need to seek professional help. There has never been a better time to do so. These disorders have become so widespread that even the smallest communities have counselors trained in these areas. You are not alone. According to the *The New England Journal of Medicine,* 1 in every 200 Americans suffers from one of these disorders.

NOBODY'S PERFECT

When I was a stockbroker, eight out of ten days were good but those two days that were bad were really bad. It reenacted "Murphy's Law." Anything that could go wrong did go wrong. No matter what. I went to the gym after work, took a nap, and then went out. But I never dwelled on the stress in my life. My mother always said, "This, too, shall pass." And it usually did. Stress is my middle name. You know the old expression, "When the going gets tough, the tough go shopping!" This is true of a lot of women, but not of me. I've never been a stress shopper. Maybe a few pairs of shoes now and then. I don't panic—I use stress to my advantage. I take every negative stressful situation and turn it into a positive situation. It's better to manage stress than to avoid it altogether. Most often an ounce of prevention will save you a lot of stress later on.

One way to prevent stress is never to make assumptions. Assumption is the mother of all "screw-ups." I always try to plan ahead and leave plenty of time to get everything done. But there are those days when whatever you do nothing seems to go right. You thought your appointment was at twelve when it was at ten-thirty; you forgot to bring the right papers to a meeting; you go to a party that was supposed to be casual in blue jeans and the other women are in cocktail dresses. You just have to laugh at yourself sometime. Never take yourself too seriously. Always remember to lighten up. When you have a bad day or a good day, treat them all the same. Don't sulk.

The stress-relieving techniques I have suggested are ones that work for me. They may work for you too. Just as each of our fingerprints is unique, so is each of our lives. If you suffer with an extreme amount of stress or feel overwhelmed by the pressures of your daily life, get help from a trained medical counselor or spiritual advisor. Part of loving ourselves is knowing when we need help. If we don't get it, our lives spin out of control, and losing weight becomes the least of our problems.

CHAPTER NINE

Move It and Lose It

"No pain, no gain–no way!"

With Stephanie Powers at Tatou in L.A.

With Julio Inglesias at the 1997 Presidential Inaugural Ball.

Exercise is not my idea of a good time. I hate to sweat. In fact, I have trouble relating to people who actually *like* to work out. My motto is, "If I can't do it in high heels, I'm not interested." But I know I have to, so I do it anyway. In a sense, we are always exercising. From the time we get up in the morning to the time we lie down at night, our bodies are in constant motion. It's simply a matter of choosing what kind and how much.

Not all exercises are equally valuable. Some, like housework, are more hard work than hard exercise; they tire you out but do little for your muscles. Others, like jogging, are high energy burners but poor muscle builders. Some forms are fun; a kiss burns 6 to 12 calories, and sex burns 350 an hour—but where are you going to find a man who can last for an hour? And even Wolfgang Puck, world-famous chef, says, "sex is dietic." What all this means is that you have to exercise smart, not just exercise hard.

You already know that exercise alone won't make you lose weight; you have to cut calories to do that.

What exercise will do is tone your body and develop and strengthen your muscles. For those of you who are wondering why you would want to increase muscle size, remember this basic fact: The more muscle you have, the more calories you burn. Muscle needs enormous amounts of calories to maintain itself. Muscle is what burns away the body fat. Have you ever watched a thin, muscular person eat and eat and eat, and never gain a pound? "If I ate like that," you think to yourself, "I'd be the size of two houses." I know; I've said it to myself.

And it's true. The overweight person has less muscle to burn fat. Cruel though it seems, it's those skinny muscular people whose bodies are fat-burning machines.

Luckily, though, the situation isn't hopeless. Anyone can build muscle, and as your own muscle mass builds through exercise, you'll find that you can eat more and more without gaining weight. If that's not motivation, I don't know what is. The ideal exercise program combines exercise regimes so that your heart will get pumped up, and your muscles will get tired down. In the process you'll not only build muscle and lose weight; you'll feel better in a dozen other ways as well. Your stress level will drop, your cardiovascular health will improve, and your lungs will handle oxygen more efficiently. These three factors combined will also increase your mental performance and, amazingly enough, actually slow down the aging process.

With this in mind, I've broken down the activities in this chapter into three types: aerobic activities, calisthenics, and resistance training. They are designed to complement one another. All the activities have health benefits and will contribute to your overall toning. They are set up in an easy progression, starting with activities so simple you won't even know you're exercising.

So now that I have you all pumped up, what do you need to do? Follow these suggestions.

BEFORE YOU EXERCISE

1. See a doctor. Even if you consider yourself perfectly healthy, it's still wise to consult your doctor before beginning an exercise program. Exercise can aggravate some medical conditions, so have your doctor check out any aches, pains, or chronic conditions you may have, however minor. This will not only ensure that you don't harm yourself; it will also give you a benchmark against which to measure your progress.

2. Plan a schedule. If your exercise program is to be effective, you must exercise regularly. You must plan to devote at least 30 minutes, three times a week, to your exercise regimen. If you don't plan for it, you won't do it. Pencil it into your schedule just as you would any other appointment.

3. Dress correctly.   God knows I like to dress fashionably, but this is the one place fashion doesn't count—function does. Appropriate clothing for exercise will offer comfort and support, without chafing. A good sports bra is a must for women. And for men and women alike, the most important item you wear will be your shoes. Shoes designed for running are not intended for aerobics; running shoes are built to absorb shock, whereas aerobic shoes are built to prevent twists and sprains. A wide variety of good-quality athletic shoes is available at reasonable prices. Find an athletic shoe store that knows its business, and invest in a good pair. You'll be investing in yourself.

4. Stretch.   Every exercise session should begin with some easy, simple stretches. Stretching is a way to wake the body up and let it know that some activity is about to begin. It is as natural as stretching before you get out of bed in the morning, to let your body know it's time to get going. Stretching moves blood into your muscles and helps to prevent injury. There are many types of stretches to choose from, but here are a few of my favorites.

A FEW SIMPLE STRETCHES

1. Quadriceps (front of thigh) stretch.   Take a standing position, holding on to a stable object with your left hand for support. Bend your right knee, reach back with your right hand, and grab your right foot or ankle. Keeping your posture erect, pull your foot gently but firmly toward your rear end. Keep your knee pointing straight down. Release and repeat on the other side, using the left hand on the left foot.

2. Calf stretch.   Stand with the balls of your feet on the edge of a step. Hold firmly to a stable fixture such as a bannister. Slowly lower one heel off the edge of the step until you feel a pulling sensation in your calf. Keep your knee straight but not locked. Slowly and carefully bend your knee straight but not locked. Slowly and carefully bend your knee slightly to shift the intensity. Repeat with the other leg.

3. Crossover stretch. Sit on the floor with your legs stretched out straight in front. Place your right hand to the side and rear of your body for support. Lift your right foot and place it on the outside of your left knee, twisting your hips slightly as you do so. Now turn your torso to the right, placing your left elbow against the outside of your right thigh and turning your head over your right shoulder as far as possible. You will feel a stretch in your upper and middle back as you do so. Return to original position, reverse the procedure, and stretch to the other side.

4. Inner thigh stretch. Sit down on the floor. Pull your knees up into a bent position and then place the soles of your feel flat against each other. Using your hands, gently push your knees outward, toward the floor. With your knees still pointing outward and your torso erect, lean forward and push down on your knees with your elbows until you feel the stretch in your inner thighs and groin.

5. Hamstring (back of thigh) stretch. Remain seated on the floor following the inner thigh stretch. Keeping one leg in the inner thigh stretch position, slowly straighten out the other leg and stretch it out to the side. Leaning forward over your straight leg, try to grab your ankle with your hands. If you can't reach your ankle, grab on to your calf. Pull your chest down toward your outstretched leg, with your back elongated, head and shoulders reaching forward, and toe pointed upward. You will feel the stretch in your leg and back. Straighten up and repeat with other leg.

6. Morning star stretch. This is Elizabeth Taylor's favorite back stretch, and she does it twice a day. Lie flat on your back on the floor. Extend your right arm over your head, and place your left arm on the floor at a 90° angle to your body. Keep your legs straight and your buttocks relaxed. Tuck your hips under, pushing the pelvis up.

Then swing your left leg over and across your right leg. Hold for 30 seconds. Repeat five times, alternating the opposite arm and leg.

AEROBIC ACTIVITIES

1. Walking.   Walking is the exercise of kings. I love it both for its simplicity and for the opportunity it gives me to get outside and enjoy the scenery. Luckily, I live in Southern California much of the year, so I can walk every day if I want to, with no fear of blizzards. Now, when I say walking, I'm not referring to window shopping on Rodeo Drive—that's a different favorite activity. I'm talking about walking at a brisk pace, say 4 miles an hour, much too fast for a good look in a shop window. A brisk walk burns off 348 calories in an hour and raises your metabolism in the process. Best of all, walking keeps your metabolism going for 2 to 3 hours after your walk is finished. This makes the perfect evening activity: take a walk after work, have a light dinner, and relax in the happy knowledge that your body is making quick work of the calories.

There are several things to remember as you begin your exercise walking. First, make sure to put on the right shoes. I strongly recommend wearing good walking shoes, which are almost as popular these days as running shoes. Your feet and back will both thank you for it.

The second thing you must remember is that this is a *walk,* not a stroll. If you are new to exercise, you should begin slowly, but after ten minutes on the road, you should pick up your pace. Walk as briskly as you can, moving your arms as you step, attacking the sidewalk rather than just gliding slowly down it. If you find yourself becoming overtired, or your legs begin to labor, relax your pace until you feel more comfortable. Your goal is to be able to maintain an aggressive pace for at least 20 minutes, so you will get the true aerobic workout you want. After the first few outings, you'll find yourself striding like a pro and receiving all the cardiovascular and weight loss benefits that this glorious form of exercise provides.

As with all forms of exercise, walking consistently is the key to success. You need to schedule a walk at least three or four times a week, 45 minutes at a time, to get the full benefits you need. According to government studies, your minimum goal should be 12 miles a week. That may sound like a very long way while you're sitting there reading this page, but you'll soon find out that 12 miles is nothing to a committed walker. Once you settle into the rhythm of regular walking, you'll soon leave that 12-mile minimum in the dust.

2. *Swimming.* If walking is the exercise of kings, swimming is the exercise of gods. There is something truly ethereal about gliding through water. Buoyed by the the crystal clear water of a pool or warm surf at the beach, your body is free of the pressure on its joints that gravity usually provides. Long recommended as a form of physical therapy, swimming is the exercise of choice for those with arthritis or back problems.

I prefer to swim in the ocean, but those of you who are geographically disadvantaged will have to settle for a pool. Consider yourself lucky if you have one of your very own. Another excellent possibility is a local swim club, school or university, or YMCA or YWCA. Many of them open their doors to the public to help and for a nominal fee you can use their facilities.

As with walking, the key to swimming aerobically is speed and distance. Remember to stretch before diving in, and allow at least a half-hour of continuous activity for optimum conditioning. You should aim for a minimum of 900 yards a week—nine lengths of an Olympic-sized pool, which will be nothing once you get into "the swim of it." You'll soon be looking like Esther Williams—or if you prefer, Whitney Houston, who recently lost 52 pounds swimming laps.

3. *Biking.* I admit it; I'm not much of a biker. It isn't that I can't pedal with the best of them. It's just that in Los Angeles or New York, weaving through traffic on a bike gives a whole new meaning to putting the pedal to the metal. You, on the other hand, may live in an area where you can pedal down the street without risking life and limb. If so, you should definitely take advantage of this excellent aerobic activity. A top leg, buttocks, and lower back conditioner, biking also provides all of the cardiovascular benefits found in walking and swimming.

As with swimming and walking, remember to stretch before beginning, and start slow. After you're warmed up, plan to ride for at least thirty continuous minutes to achieve optimum aerobic benefit. Your goal is to ride a minimum of 24 miles per week, which will be easy once you get whizzing along. One piece of advice: Don't switch to a higher gear while pedaling if you don't need to. Although gearing up will force your thigh and buttocks muscles to work harder, your cadence will decrease significantly. Struggling to pedal will sacrifice leg speed, and put your knees under unnecessary strain. The key to aerobic biking is an easier (lower) gear, which forces you to pedal more quickly. On the other hand, remember that downhill stretches aren't an excuse to rest. Don't just coast down the hills; put your bike in high gear and keep on pedaling. Coasting is fun, but it's definitely not exercise.

As for those of you who love indoor biking—at the risk of offending you, I have to say that cycling indoors is like reading in the dark. You end up missing most of the fun while intensifying the difficulty. I realize that many of you are tried-and-true bikers whose entire concept of aerobic exercise is long stretches in the health club on a stationary cycle. And I'll admit that a stationary cycle is probably the safest choice if you live in a big city. But for those of you who can ride safely outside, the benefits of fresh air and natural surroundings beat the inside of a sweaty health club hands down. So does the changing scenery outside, which makes the time spent on a bike seem to fly by. But for those of you who do elect to bike indoors, don't forget to stretch first and adjust the gears so your legs can pump at a brisk pace. Strap on your helmet, and enjoy your ride. Instant gratification.

4. Aerobics.   Pull on your tights and crank up the music! If you're like me, you love to move to the beat of good music. Whether in a class or at home, aerobics is so much like dancing that you may forget you're exercising. Because I love to dance, aerobics is a reward in itself.

If you prefer the social atmosphere of a dance class as I do, you won't have much difficulty finding one. Every health club, school, and community center seems to have one these days. Before you sign up for a long-term commitment, though, take a look at both the facility and the instructor. You need to make sure the floor you'll be bouncing on is cushioned wood (a sprung floor is best), not wood over concrete—or worse still, plain concrete. Jumping up and down on the wrong kind of floor can do serious damage to your joints. You also need to make sure the instructor is someone you'll enjoy working out with. There are usually plenty of classes to choose from, so if you don't like the look of the floor or the teacher, move on to the next place.

Once you've found a facility you like and signed up, the next step is to get the right clothes. As with walking and running, wearing the right shoes is crucial. All the sports shoe manufacturers make shoes designed for aerobics, and it's well worth investing in a pair. Unlike running shoes, which are designed to absorb road shock, aerobic shoes are designed to protect you from twisted ankles and knees during those side-to-side maneuvers. Don't take class without them.

Once you're dressed and ready to go, don't forget to stretch before you get started. The instructor will have you stretch at the beginning of class, but those extra few minutes of stretching before class starts will make your body even more prepared. You can expect a good class to last 45 minutes to an hour, including at least 10 minutes of stretching, 20 to 30 minutes of low-impact aerobic dance, and a cooldown. You'll leave with your heart pumping and your metabolism cruising along at peak performance.

If the thought of bouncing around in a room full of strangers isn't your idea of a good time, purchase a home video to pop into the VCR. The aerobic home videos inspired by Jane Fonda have turned into a cottage industry. Get several and rotate them so you won't get bored without an instructor there to pump you up in person. Be especially careful to wear the right shoes and choose a safe surface for your home workout. Also be careful to follow the form modeled by your video instructor. Without a real live instructor in the room with you, your chances of injury escalate if you're careless.

5. Jogging.   Once the health craze of the eighties, jogging is still the exercise of choice for high-profile people like Oprah Winfrey, who's achieved an incredible level of fitness. Be that as it may, there is still nothing I'm less interested in doing than pulling on a pair of sweatpants and jogging on a treadmill, or worse yet, down the sidewalks of Beverly Hills. I'm in good company when it comes to my distrust of jogging. The National Centers for Disease Control confirm that one in three joggers who run 6 or more miles a week will sustain injury. The high impact of the jogger's stride, especially on city cement, can pound away at every bodily joint and put particular pressure on the hips, knees, ankles, and feet. In other words, jogging has the potential to do the runner more harm than good. And although no government agency will back me up on this one, I strongly suspect that jogging makes every body part a woman owns sag before its time. So if you must jog, be sure to stretch thoroughly first, and buy top-quality, good-fitting shoes.

CALISTHENICS

Our word "calisthenics" is made up from two Greek words which mean "beautiful strength." The following calisthenic exercises take general aerobics one step further by concentrating their motion on a particular group of muscles, with the idea in mind of strengthening and toning them. Also like aerobic activities, these exercises—if done vigorously enough to raise your heart rate—will help curb the appetite. While aerobic activities crank up the metabolism and help to burn fat, these exercises will help to reshape your muscles into beautiful perfection.

The following calisthenics are designed to be done as a set. Performed correctly and completely, this group of exercises will tighten your body from head to toe, and give you a moderate cardiovascular workout at the same time. As with any form of exercise, don't forget to stretch thoroughly before you begin.

1. Abdominal crunch. On both men and women, a tight, firm stomach is the first sign of a toned body. Unfortunately, the classic sit-up is the least effective way of achieving the result we all want. We all did them in PE class—you lie on the floor, put your hands behind your head, and bring your elbows to your knees. You end up straining your back and neck and putting excessive pressure on your hip-flexor muscles, all with minimal effect on your abdominal muscles. The abdominal crunch, on the other hand, is the perfect way to achieve the tight, toned abdominal muscles you long for.

Follow these instructions, and you'll be doing the most effective abdominal exercise around.

Lie down on the carpet or an exercise mat. Keeping your lower back firmly on the floor, bend your knees at a 45° angle to isolate the abdominal muscles. Keep your feet flat on the floor, 6 inches apart, a foot or so from your buttocks. Cross your arms across your chest, resting your fingers lightly on your shoulders. Let your elbows rest comfortably against your sides, where they'll stay.

Now lift *only* your shoulders and upper back, leaving your lower back on the floor. Curl your shoulders up and forward, tightening your abs as you do so. The amount of actual motion will be relatively small; your shoulders should rise enough so that your shoulder blades come off the floor. The idea is to curl up like a cocktail shrimp. At the top of the motion, your chin will be tucked up against your chest; at the bottom, you uncurl and relax your neck. Hold the crunch position for a few seconds; then take another few seconds to slowly lower back down. Exhale as you curl up and inhale as you curl down. Repeat ten times for one full set. Rest a full minute; then repeat until you've done a total of three sets.

If you've done this exercise correctly, you'll feel the results immediately. That burning sensation in your midsection is your proof that the muscle fibers are building. Believe me, a few of these are infinitely more effective than the old-fashioned sit-up, and without the damage to your back.

2. Give me an R. The name of this exercise comes from the days when cheerleaders performed it on a playing field. It is also called the circle stretch, and it works the abdominal muscles as well as your internal and external obliques on each side. It goes like this.

Stand with your feet spread shoulder-width apart, and your hands raised over your head so that your body forms an "X"—the classic cheerleader stance. Bending at the waist, curl your arms and shoulders to the right until your torso and arms are at right angles to the floor. You should feel a stretch on your *left* side. Hold the stretch for 5 seconds; then reverse the motion, moving your arms to the left side, parallel to the floor. You have now completed a half-circle, from your right side to your left. Repeat the circular motion, alternating sides, until you have stretched both sides five times each. This is one set. Rest a minute; then repeat two more sets.

3. Leg raises. This is the exercise that movie legend Marlene Dietrich is rumored to have done for General George Patton during World War II. While it might not have sped up the end of the war, it undoubtedly made General Patton's day, and helped make Dietrich's legs the stuff of legends. Here's how you get legendary legs for yourself.

Lie on a carpet or exercise mat on your right side. Extend your legs straight out, knees together. Stretch your right arm straight out on the floor and rest your head comfortably on it. Place your left hand on the floor in front of you as a stabilizer. Keeping it straight, lift your left leg to a 45° angle. Hold it there for 1 second; then lower it slowly down. Repeat ten times, switch to your left side, and repeat. When you have completed both sides, you will have done one full set. Rest 2 minutes and repeat, completing three sets.

4. Inner thighs. For both men and women, the inner thighs are fat collectors. This exercise pinpoints the problem area with bull's eye accuracy.

Lie on your left side. Extend your left arm and rest your head on it, forming a smooth, continuous line with your body. Put your right leg over your left, placing your right foot flat on the floor. Make sure that your hips are aligned at a 90° angle to the floor, and then tighten your abdominal muscles. With your right foot still planted firmly on the floor for balance, lift and lower your *left* leg on and off the floor. You will not be able to lift the leg far, but you will most definitely feel it. By the time you complete 12 lifts, your inner thigh should be burning. Turn over and repeat on the other side. This is one complete set. Rest a minute; then repeat one more set.

5. Torso twists. For those of you who wake up with stiffness every morning, the torso twist is a lifesaver. It is a wonderful way to stretch the waist, back, and shoulders.

Stand straight, feet shoulder-width apart. Extend your arms up and out to your sides at shoulder level, parallel to the floor. Rotate your shoulders to the left; then bend and touch your right hand to your left foot. Straighten to your original position and reverse, touching the left hand to the right toe. Repeat, touching each toe ten times. This is one complete set. Rest; then repeat two more complete sets.

6. Back extensors.   The perfect way to cool you down, these extensors not only work the back but enhance the buttocks as well.

Lie on your stomach, on the carpet or exercise mat. Extend your arms straight in front, with your legs straight in back. Open your arms and legs to form an "X." Tighten your buttocks. Slowly lift your right arm and left leg off the floor. Hold and release. Repeat ten times. Then switch sides, lifting your left arm and right leg ten times. This is one complete set. Rest a minute; then complete two more sets, resting between each.

7. Stretch and cool-down.   This is the best part of calisthenics. You've done the hard work; now you're ready to slowly stretch out your muscles to prevent cramping, and allow your heart rate to gradually return to normal.

From your last "X" position on the floor, bring your arms together overhead; then bring your legs together. Slowly push yourself up into a sitting position on your knees, *rolling* your back out as you do so. If you've ever seen a cat get up from a nap, you know the motion. With your hands to give a little extra help, slowly rise to your feet, once again rolling your back as you rise to your standing position. Relax your neck and let your head roll around in a circle, first to the left, then to the right, relaxing your muscles as you do so. This should feel wonderful. Finally, put your hands together in front of your body and give yourself a hand for a job well done.

RESISTANCE EXERCISES

Entire books have been written on weight lifting and muscle building. I have no intention of trying to duplicate that effort. The purpose of this section is simply to give you a basic exercise routine that you can do at home using hand-held weights. (Notice I say "weights"; if the term "dumbbell" isn't politically incorrect by now, it should be). It is important for both men and women to work out with weights. Women shouldn't fear becoming muscle-bound; our natural estrogen levels prevent this, just as men's testosterone levels build thicker, broader muscles.

The added weight in your exercise routine will provide the extra resistance you need to strain down your muscle cells. This may sound like a bad thing, but the fact is that when you do, your body will strengthen them with improved models that are stronger, tighter, and more efficient than the old ones. It is this continuing process of straining and strengthening your muscles that will gradually alter muscle shape and size. If you keep a steady pace to your weight routine, you may also give your body a good aerobic workout at the same time.

Nearly every muscle group in the body can be exercised and strengthened with hand-held free weights. Because they are easy to control, a slight shift in position or range of motion can target different parts of muscle groups for an incredibly effective workout. Not only are the weights endlessly adaptable to changing regimens; they are inexpensive, inconspicuous, and nearly indestructible. Before you leap into action, though, you need to determine how heavy your hand-held weight should be. Women typically use a lighter weight than men. I suggest women should begin with two to five pound weights. Men can often start with ten pounds or more. For both men and women, however, heavier is not necessarily better. When you're beginning, it's better to do more repetitions with a light weight than to do fewer with a heavy one. By buying adjustable weights, you can start as light as you have to, and add weight as you gain strength.

The following set of exercises will provide you with a full-body workout. They're designed to be done in the order listed, starting with the largest muscle groups so that you can complete the full body range without becoming completely exhausted. Remember to use steady, smooth movements, and to aim for eight to twelve repetitions per set. You can start off by doing one set of each exercise, and add a set each week until you get to three sets. If you find you can do more, increase your weight. And as always, be sure to stretch before getting started.

1. The lunge.   This is one of the best exercises you can do to keep your tush from sagging. With a weight in each hand, stand erect with your back straight and your feet about a foot apart. Your arms should be relaxed and hang at your sides. Take a giant step forward with your right foot. Your left foot should stay put (although your heel will roll up), as your leg stretches out behind you. Your left knee will be nearly on the floor. The posture looks something like a fencer's lunge, except that your feet are parallel, and your arms down. Your weight should be centered on the heel of your forward foot. Hold this position for a couple of seconds and then push yourself upright, concentrating your effort on your forward leg. As you push up, exhale. Now, repeat for the other side. Alternating sides, do ten to twelve repetitions. If you have trouble keeping your balance, don't worry— it takes a few times to get the hang of it. Your buns will love you for the effort.

2. Calf raises. You'll need an aerobic step or some other 4 inch platform to do this exercise. Position the platform at a right angle to a wall. Steady yourself against the wall with your left hand, and holding a weight in your right, step up on the platform with your right foot. The ball of your foot should be on the platform, with your heel hanging over the edge. Hold your left foot up off the ground, or wrap it around your right ankle—whatever feels comfortable to you. Keep your back straight, and rise up on the toes of your right foot, contracting your calf muscle. Hold the position for a couple of seconds, and slowly let yourself back down. If you let your heel drop below the level of the step, you'll get a nice stretch. Do ten to twelve repetitions, then turn around and do the other leg.

3. Side bends. This exercise is for the muscles that are under those love handles. Hold a weight in your right hand and place your left hand on your hip. Lean to the right as far as you can, while keeping your torso straight—not leaning forward or backward. The weight will help pull you down. Return to the upright position and then bend to the left pulling against the weight. This is one repetition. Do ten to twelve repetitions, then repeat for the other side (remember to switch hands with the weight).

4. Leg lifts. Skip this exercise if you have a bad back. If your back is okay, this will both build strength and enhance flexibility in the hamstrings and lower back. Stand straight with your feet shoulder width apart and your weights in front of you, at your feet. Bend at the waist and your back flat. Slowly stand up, punching with your quadriceps (front thighs), and buttocks. Do not use your back to lift. exhale as you lift, to tighten up your abdominal muscles and support your back. Return the weights to the floor, assuming the squatting position again. This is one repetition. Do eight to twelve repetitions.

5. Flat press. This is an exercise for your major pectoral, or chest, muscles. Sagging chest muscles aren't flattering for either men or women. This exercise won't give women bigger breasts, but it will strengthen the muscles and ligaments that help support them. This exercise requires a bench (preferably a padded exercise bench). Lie on your back on the bench, with your feet on the floor, and a weight in each hand. To start, bring the weights in close to your sides with your elbows pointing down. As you exhale, push the weights up over your chest, extending your arms fully until the weights touch at the top. Lower the weights down to the starting position. The motion simulates an old-fashioned push-up, but instead of pushing your body away from the floor, you're pushing the weights away from your body. Do eight to twelve repetitions.

6. Triceps extension. This exercise works the upper back of the arm. Women, in particular, seem to develop wings on the back of their arms. This is a combination of flabby muscles and sagging fat. This will firm up the muscle, but it won't get rid of the fat—you'll need the Star Diet to do that. You can sit on a chair or bench for this exercise. With your back straight, and a weight in your right hand, raise your right arm up toward the ceiling, with your palm facing in toward your head. This is the starting position. Bending your arm at the elbow, lower the weight down toward your back, next to and behind your head. When the weight is lowered all the way down, your elbow should still be pointing straight up at the ceiling. Now raise the weight back up to where you started. Don't let your elbow drop! This is one repetition. Repeat for eight to twelve repetitions, then switch sides.

7. Concentration curl. This exercise will tone the biceps. If you are wearing a tank top or sleeveless blouse—or a strapless evening gown—concentration curls will help you develop upper arms with that firm, athletic look. This exercise is performed in a seated position, with a slightly rounded back, a posture reminiscent of Rodin's famous sculpture, *The Thinker*. Sit on an exercise bench or chair with your feet flat on the floor and your knees a comfortable distance apart. Hold a weight in your right hand, palm up. Place your elbow on the inside of your right thigh, and let the weight dangle between your legs. Put your left hand on your knee for support, and slowly curl your right arm upward toward your right shoulder. Keep your right elbow planted against your thigh through the whole range of motion. At the top of the motion contract the muscle, feeling the flex in your biceps. Repeat for eight to twelve repetitions, then switch sides.

8. Pullovers. This exercise works another, smaller set of muscles in your chest. It was the exercise of choice for Mae West, whose Boticelli breasts needed all the muscular support they could get. Lie on your back on an exercise bench. The top of your head should be even with the end of the bench, and your feet flat on the floor. Take a single weight and hold it high over your head, using both hands. This is the starting position. Slowly lower the weight over and behind your head, extending your arms the whole time, until the weight is behind and slightly below your head. Slowly return the weight to the upright position, feeling the stretch and contraction in your chest muscles. Repeat the exercise for eight to twelve repetitions.

9. Shoulder presses. This exercise is sometimes called the military press, and works the muscles in the shoulders and upper back. Take a weight in each hand, knuckles facing up and palms forward, as though you were hanging on to a chin-up bar. Standing straight, with your feet comfortably apart and your knees slightly bent, extend your hands up over your head, hold for one count, and bring them back down. Don't cheat and use your legs or arch your back to get a little extra oomph. Concentrate on using your shoulders to do the lift. Repeat for eight to twelve repetitions.

10. Lateral raises. This exercise works the deltoids, the triangular-shaped muscle group located where the upper arms and outer part of the shoulders meet. You don't have too much leverage when you do this exercise, so you will probably have to use a light weight. Hold a weight in each hand, with your arms down at your sides, palms facing in. Exhale as you raise your arms up and out to the side. At the top of the motion your hands will be slightly higher than your shoulders—don't go any higher—and straight out to the sides. Let them down slowly as you inhale. An alternate form of this exercise, which works the front "head" of the deltoid, is to lift the weights straight forward, away from your body to the front. Repeat for eight to twelve repetitions.

TIME OUT

If there's one comment I hear from people who are out of shape, it's "I don't have time to work out." And every time I hear it, my reaction is the same. From Fabio to Joan Collins to Ivana Trump, each one of my celebrity friends runs a business, manages a career, cares for family and friends, and *still finds time to exercise*. Each one of them is in incredible shape. In fact, by alloting time to exercise every day, they create more time for other things. Their fitness level not only keeps them looking great; it gives them the energy to accomplish their other tasks at record speed.

If you really want to work out, you'll find the time. You must make a commitment to yourself to schedule exercise time every day. You'll look better, feel better, and get more done. The following weekly schedule works well for most beginners. After a while, you'll develop an agenda of your own.

Day 1: Aerobic activities (walking, swimming, etc.)
Day 2: Resistance training (weight lifting)
Day 3: Calisthenics—stretching and toning
Day 4: Rest (shopping)
Day 5: Aerobic activities (dancing)
Day 6: Resistance training (or swimming)
Day 7: Resting

You'll see that I've mixed activities, not only for maximum physical benefit, but to minimize boredom. Don't let things get too predictable; mix your routine as your mood (and the weather) suggest.

One last bit of advice: If you regularly participate in a favorite sport, by all means keep it in your schedule. Do *not,* however, consider it a replacement for your exercise regimen. Too often in sports, the body is given time to rest and slow down breathing. This defeats the aerobic benefit of the activity. Aerobic activity must be continuous. Your goal is to burn fat and develop a strong and healthy heart, lungs, and body. Your favorite sport may be great relaxation, but it will not give you the benefits a regular exercise regimen will. Besides, just think what all that working out will do for your golf swing!

TIPS TO REMEMBER

1. Schedule.   Make an appointment to exercise and keep it.

2. Warm up.   Stretching improves flexibility, helps prevent injury, and prepares you for exercise.

3. No pain, no gain . . . no way.   This old saying is a leftover from smelly locker rooms. Your muscles should ache, but they shouldn't scream. If they do, you're doing something wrong.

4. Drink fluids.   One by-product of exercise is perspiration. Replenish your body fluids with water often to prevent dehydration.

5. Cool down.   Cooling down is every bit as important as warming up. The cool-down allows your heart rate to return to normal gradually. Your metabolism will still remain elevated for at least 2 hours after exercising, providing you with extra burn power for your Star Diet meals.

CHAPTER TEN

StarCaps®: The Celebrity Secret

*"Some people are no good at counting calories
and have figures to prove it."*

With David Charvet in L.A.

At a party with Tony Curtis.

tarCaps. Even the name is tantalizing. Those who've tried them call them "nothing short of miraculous, a magic potion in a bottle." Never one for false modesty, I have to agree. From the time I created StarCaps 15 years ago and took my first capsule, I knew I had found something that was going to change my dieting habits forever. As the FenPhen controversy proved once again, you take diet drugs at your own risk. I should know. I spent my teenage years in the goldfish bowl known as Beverly Hills High School (90210, the most famous zip code in the world), home of the rich and land of the gorgeous and the thin. At the time i wasn't grossly overweight, but I thought I was. Anything over a size 4 was too much in the slim and sleek crowd surrounding me. I needed to lose twenty pounds to get down to a size I could live with. When fretting and starving didn't work, I turned to diet pills—amphetamines, to be exact. In those days they were dispensed like candy by "diet doctors" who have long since been put out of business. These "medical experts" practiced a form of diet counseling that was chemically fueled and widely available.

I took, the pills on and off for years. When I got married, my husband was against them right from the start. This didn't mean I stopped taking them, mind you. It only meant that I took them on the q.t. Unfortunately, when you take amphetamines, you can't keep it a secret for long. After I had painted the apartment, washed the car, and mowed the lawn before lunch, he knew.

It didn't matter that I kept denying it. My hyperactivity combined with my irritability were red flags that little Nikki had been in the pill jar again. I was not only hurting my health and my marriage, the darn things didn't even work. Oh, sure I lost weight while I was on the pills. As soon as I stopped, I ate everything in sight. (And why not? I had been starving myself to death!)

Then I began my StarCaps regime. Let me stress that StarCaps are not diet pills. They don't kill your appetite. They have no nicotine, thyroid, caffeine, or amphetamines in them. They are not the magic bullet, but close to it.

StarCaps the all-natural dietary supplement, is a unique blend of natural plant principals designed to supplement a well-balanced diet. The natural principals include papaya containing papain, a plant enzyme, and a specially processed extract of fresh garlic.

There are those who have tried to duplicate my garlic papaya blend on their own, to no avail. When I say that it is a unique garlic and a special papaya, I'm not kidding. The garlic used in StarCaps is called "macho garlic" and is only grown in the fertile Andes mountains near Arequipa, Peru. It's black and much larger than the garlic which flavors your favorite marinara sauce. This special garlic is a natural diuretic (a fact confirmed with your first capsule or two). And because of its incredible potency, we carefully dry and deodorize the garlic.

The papaya, too, comes from Peru. Grown in the tropical rain forests along the Amazon River, the papaya is carefully dried to retain the enzyme activity of the natural papain it contains. It's the action of the papain and garlic which helps metabolize protein and fat and detox your system.

The medicinal properties of garlic and papaya are legendary. In ancient Rome and Greece, the garlic clove was revered for its ability to heal and stave off illness.

Modern science has enabled us to understand what the ancients knew only by experience. Researchers have broken down the components of garlic to provide concrete evidence that garlic is more than just tasty flavoring. They've found that in addition to water, carbohydrates, protein, fiber, essential amino acids, and the vitamins and minerals found in most vegetables, garlic contains organosulfur compounds that give it its distinctive flavor and odor. When the garlic clove is crushed, the odorless amino acid allin is converted to allicin, a liquid with amazing antibacterial properties.

It is the allicin in garlic which helps to ward off colds and other infections in the bloodstream as well as detoxing the system as a whole. It's function as a free radical scavenger has been scientifically documented. A medical study published in 1992 by the University of Limburg in the Netherlands suggests that garlic is significant in preventing cancer in both humans and laboratory animals. The garlic in StarCaps provides an especially high percentage of allicin, enhancing your natural immunity against illness while helping you lose weight. Although Star Dieters use StarCaps[R] primarily for their diuretic properties, their ability to help the body fight disease is an important bonus. The healthier you are, the easier it will be to maintain a desirable weight.

Papaya, the other primary ingredient in StarCaps, has been called positively magical for its ability to metabolize both fat and protein. It would be difficult to overstate the impact papaya has on your entire system. Papain, the main ingredient in papaya, is effective in breaking down fatty tissue and is often user used to tenderize tough meat.

There's another active ingredient in StarCaps—valerian. Valerian is a flowering herb whose root was first used by the ancient Greek physician Dioscorides in the first century as a relaxant. To this day, valerian's reputation as a sedative is undisputed. It is added to StarCaps to help calm the stomach as the power of the garlic and papaya begin their work.

StarCaps are easy to make part of your everyday routine. You take one a day in the morning for the first two days to allow your system to adjust. Then, you take two a day, either in the morning or mid afternoon with orange or cranberry juice or a potassium supplement. Because of the mild diuretic properties of the special garlic in StarCaps your body will be releasing excess fluid on a regular basis. This can result in loss of potassium in your system. Replenishing that potassium is important to prevent muscle cramps. That's why I recommend taking StarCaps with orange or cranberry juice, which are a good sources of potassium. Other excellent food sources of potassium are spinach, bananas, melons, prunes, dates, and raisins.

When I first created the StarCaps and started taking them, I was astonished by their effectiveness. I lost 5 pounds within days. Surprised and excited, I was so encouraged by my initial weight loss that I began to monitor my food intake more carefully than I ever had. The motivation the StarCaps offered me was almost as important as the physical effects. After two and a half weeks on the StarCaps and the diet, I had lost 18 pounds, and I felt wonderful. It was amazing to take something that actually worked. Even more important, I had no desire to overeat the moment the weight was off. Fifteen years later, those 18 pounds are still off my body. I continue to take StarCaps every day. The great thing about StarCaps is that not only can you lose weight easily, but once you've achieved the weight loss you want, if you continue to take the StarCaps and eat healthfully, they will keep you from gaining it back. A perfect way to maintain your weight.

Soon the word began to spread. My celebrity friends were dying to try the StarCaps, too. One person was supermodel Beverly Johnson, who told me, "I was doing the runway couture shows in Paris for the first time in several years, and was petrified I wouldn't be able to fit into the minuscule clothes. Nikki gave me some StarCaps, and the result was I dropped ten pounds like lightning and looked sensational. Now, I give them to my daughter Anansia, who has lost weight, too." My friend singer Lorna Luft lost even more. She had gained a lot of weight with her first baby, and she needed to lose 30 pounds after her son was born. I delivered a supply of StarCaps to the health-conscious Lorna, and she was able to drop the pounds safely and naturally. Always one to share, she told her sister Liza Minnelli and a string of friends about StarCaps; they told their friends, and the word spread from there. Soon I had a thriving business on my hands. Thousands of men and women all over the country were thrilled to find they were losing weight quickly and naturally. They're still taking them today. Traci Bingham, one of the beautiful stars of *Baywatch,* says, "Nikki Haskell's StarCaps and diet are absolutely amazing! I am a firm believer in products that work together. With StarCaps and Nikki's diet, you lose weight, keep it off, and actually see a difference. Being on *Baywatch* and wearing a skimpy swimsuit all day really makes you aware of your body. Everybody in the world looks at you and it's important to keep your figure looking right. Since I found StarCaps, I know I can never be without them. I store them next to my toothbrush and I also keep the StarSuckers candy in my purse. Thank God for StarCaps or I couldn't ever be seen in that little red suit."

Will you lose weight on the Star Diet without StarCaps? Of course, you will. It will just take you longer. However, if you do make StarCaps part of your dietary routine, your weight loss will be greatly accelerated. Taking the StarCaps dietary supplement will help you reach your ideal weight more quickly. More important, StarCaps will help you keep the weight off. As any veteran dieter knows, the only thing harder than losing the weight is keeping it off. A maintenance dose of one or two capsules a day (it varies by individual) will help keep your body permanently slim.

Even when I have dieting under control, I've always found it difficult to avoid that four o'clock sugar craving. One day, I was on the phone with my girlfriend Nancy Davis Rickel and we started discussing one of our favorite topics, dieting. Nancy said, "Wouldn't it be fabulous if there was a dietetic candy that tasted great and killed your appetite?" And that's how the StarSuckers were born.

If you are a snacker, or you have a sweet tooth, it's time to try my new diet candy products. All my diet candy products are bioengineered foods that taste great, satisfy the craving for something sweet and flavorful, and actually help suppress your appetite. They look and taste like high-calorie, high-fat candy, but they're not! They are a new kind of food called "nutraceuticals," because they have health and medical benefits, and no unhealthy ingredients.

These products are my StarSuckers, StarSucker Sours, and StarRoles. They have only 10 calories apiece; are fat-free, sugar-free, cholesterol-free, sodium-free, and lactose-free; and taste delicious. My new delicious diet chocolate candy bars, NikkiBars, have only 20 calories, and are sugar-free.

All of my candies contain my invention, Nikki Haskell's StarBlend,™ with several important proprietary ingredients including garcinia cambogia (a mild appetite suppressant and fat blocker), Korean and Siberian ginseng, royal jelly, and chromium picolinate (a blood sugar stabilizer and anti oxidant).

NikkiBars were the official snack of the 1997 Oscar De La Hoya vs. Hector Camacho welterweight championship fight in Las Vegas. NikkiBars have also been photographed by photographer Harry Langdon and painted by Peter Max, one of the great living artists of our day.

CHAPTER ELEVEN

I Look Great ... I Feel Great ... So Where's the Party?

"Smile—it uses calories."

Michael Jackson and me at Studio 54.

With Imelda Marcos at the Presidential Palace in Manila.

With Andy Warhol and Cornelia Guest on her sixteenth birthday at Le Club.

Jennie McCarthy and me with Donald Trump in Palm Beach.

Congratulations! You've made it through the diet trenches and are still with me. If you've been seriously following the Star Diet, you already know the dramatic change it has made in your appearance. If you're just getting motivated, my advice is simple—stop the excuses; start the Star Diet System; and get on with your life.

How well we know the ugly cycle. When you're out of shape and not eating correctly, your self-esteem has the depth of a puddle. Once you've lost the weight and allowed your body to function at its peak, you're equipped to go anywhere—from skiing down the slopes in San Moritz to being invited to the Oval Office at the White House. Don't think it's impossible. I've done it; and so can you. Nothing is out of our reach. That "A-list" invitation—whatever that means to you—may be waiting in the mailbox at this very moment. The key is to be prepared when it arrives.

You've worked hard to look like a million bucks; now it's time to strut your stuff. There's an old proverb that says, "There is no point in dancing in a closet." So—get out and circulate. My mother used to say, "You'll never meet anyone staying at home." Even if you have to grab a friend, a relative, or a business associate, do it. Get out the door and get in the habit of getting out in the real world.

OUT AND ABOUT

Sometimes, this is easier said than done, particularly for a single person. In reality, the easiest way to be invited out is to begin by inviting others in. Male or female, it makes no difference. Throw a party to celebrate your new look. This is a perfect opportunity to show off the new and slender you. You'll be surprised how quickly you get that first return invitation yourself. Take a trip with a friend who knows more people and places than you do.

Before you leap into your new social life, a few words of caution. I've been fortunate enough to have rubbed elbows (and other body parts) with the world's most famous, glamorous, cultivated, and notorious hosts and hostesses. From Madame Marcos to Ivana Trump, they all share one thing in common. They know how to make a guest feel that they are the most important person on the face of the planet. This is not as easy as it seems.

THE PERFECT INVITATION

For starters, it is important to be well organized. Always send a written invitation spelling out exactly why you're inviting your guests. Is it for lunch, brunch, dinner, cocktails, a bridal shower, or a weekend in the country? In today's busy society, the telephone invite is certainly more common. That does *not* mean that it's correct. If you must phone, always follow up with a note of confirmation or at least a fax. I have some friends who are so organized, they not only call and send invites, they do it 6 months in advance to ensure that you save the date. It never hurts to plan ahead. You'd be surprised how many parties are doomed before they even start because the hostess never mastered this art.

This doesn't mean that they always have to be planned within an inch of your life. Some of my best parties have been spur-of-the-moment events. I've called people an hour before, invited them over for a bite, and ended up having the hottest event in town.

In extending the invitation, don't just indicate the reason for the event; spell out the length of time they are expected to stay—come for an afternoon of tennis; come for dinner; stay the weekend, the month, the year. Always be sure to mention if your guests should come alone, bring a guest, bring the family, the pets, the neighbors.

If you receive an invitation that does not specify whom you should bring, come alone. If you don't know the protocol, call your hostess and check if you are expected alone or with a guest.

Being organized also means inviting guests who complement one another. Make certain that you don't extend invitations to two people who have just had a major split in a business relationship, a marriage on the rocks, or an affair. And never, ever, invite the ex-boyfriend or ex-girlfriend of one of your favorite newlyweds. It's not a pretty scene.

Sometimes, when you're just emerging from your fat cocoon, guests are in short supply. Initially, expect to have to include people who knew you in the old days of skin folds and blubber. Use the moment wisely. Although they may not eventually fit into your new circle of friends, they most certainly can serve an excellent purpose now. There is nothing like seeing the shock on the face of someone who knew you before your transformation. It makes all the sacrifice and hard work worthwhile. And there is no better source for compliments of the new, trim, and vibrant you than people who knew you when.

THE ROYAL FLASH

It's always nice to have a prince or princess in the group. Now, before you think that I lost my mind when I lost my weight, the concept may seem foreign to you now, but it isn't as hard as you may think. There's an excess of Yugoslavian royalty these days, and they can be found in the unlikeliest places. And the Italians have more contessas than pizzas. Movie stars, singers, or at the very least, former stars from your favorite television shows of the sixties also add pizzazz.

If you're short on kings, and Meryl Streep hasn't been introduced in your circle as yet, go through your list and invite the best of the lot. A tycoon or two is always nice. Every town, no matter how small, has a tycoon (he runs the local bank or brokerage firm), an intellectual (the librarian), a movie star (the drama teacher), and a few socialites (the wife of the owner of the bank and her friends). It's always good to throw in someone who is deliciously naughty as well as one who is deliciously nice. Often they turn out to be the same person.

TRAVEL EQUIPMENT

There are other cardinal rules as well. Always let your guests know beforehand if they should bring a special outfit or costume. No use planning a masked ball if everyone only packs hiking gear. If it's black tie, spell it out. Also, describe the transportation so that overnight guests may rent a car, a seaplane, a gondola, a sleigh, or whatever is appropriate in your locale.

In the same mood, remind guests about any special supplies they may need—mosquito netting, thermal underwear, bungee-jumping equipment, a parachute, swim fins, etc. One time I houseguested with my then-boyfriend, Gerry Goldsmith, at Edgar Bronfman's (the Seagram's heir) hunting lodge on a private island in Canada. He forgot to inform one of the female guests that we were going on a "rough-it weekend." She was quite a standout in her hot pants, leopard tights, and stiletto pumps. On top of everything else, her suede coat, which wasn't warm enough to begin with, fell into the Saint Lawrence River!

SOCIAL SECURITY

Always, always notify guests if wild animals roam the premises at night. This includes dogs and cats, just in case your guest is sensitive to assault or allergies. And please make a point of indicating any special security arrangements. No need to set off alarms that will summon the local authorities. Once I was staying with a girlfriend of mine in her luxurious penthouse apartment in Paris. On the way out of the door for dinner, I pushed what I thought was the light switch. It was the panic intrusion button. She was unfortunately sleeping when several policemen with loaded guns broke down her front door.

Joan Schnitzer, who ranks as one of the consummate Texas hostesses, has her own way of handling the situation. She informed me when I stayed at her home in Houston that I would be locked in my room and not allowed out until eight the next morning. Sure enough, when the security system was turned on, the bolts slid shut with the precision of Attica.

Don't Eat That

As the perfect hostess, don't forget to make sure that you ask your guests about foods which are not acceptable. Everyone has something they either can't, or won't, eat or drink. This is more than just a courtesy, you will soon discover. By planning seemingly impromptu meals, you do more than keep control over your guests' diet. You keep control over your own. Remember that entertaining and dieting should go hand in hand. Where food is concerned, spell it out. Leaving guests on their own for uncatered lunches or dinners can only lead to tragedy. Somehow they *always* find the caviar or that special bottle of wine you were saving a *truly* special occasion.

Elements of Surprises

People never seem to outgrow their love for party favors. It starts with your first party at your friend's fourth birthday and continues through life. The competition for the best favors at the top parties is fierce. Large or small, party favors are a way of making your guest feel special and glad they came. This is another area where you can put your creativity to work.

Over the years, I have always decorated the tables of my birthday parties with little wind-up toys, dice, jacks, toy cars, sunglasses—you name it. I also throw in a few bottles of StarCaps. By the end of the party, the tables are empty and my guests' purses are filled to the brim. There is nothing they like more than taking home cute souvenirs.

I have a friend, Dennis Basso, who gave a very chic dinner party and decorated the tables with his lifelong collection of crystal glass. They took those too! Unfortunately, they weren't supposed to. If you put it on the table, "they will take it". So be careful! The last thing you need to lose is your mother's favorite antiques.

The rich and famous love to be generous with their little tokens. When Madame Marcos entertained house guests, she always made sure they received little presents on their nightstand every evening when they retired. Little candies, a schedule of the next day's activities, and an autographed picture of her and the President.

When Ivana Trump was still married to Donald, she hosted her famous spa weekends at their grand palace Mar-a-Lago in Palm Beach, Florida, (the former home of Marjorie Merriweather Post which is considered to be one of the great estates of the world). Ivana treated her invited girlfriends to a full schedule of exercise classes, massage, manicure, pedicure and hair appointments. As one of the great hostesses, Ivana's special touch was an amenities kit that included a gold toothbrush and razor. Now Donald has turned the Mar-a-Lago into a club. The initiation fees are a whopping $75,000.00 and Mar-a-Lago is considered one of the greatest spas in the country today.

LITTLE THINGS MEAN A LOT

Ironically, I have found that the littlest things are the ones that stay in the memories of your guests the longest. You can plan the biggest dinner party, serve the most expensive champagne, have sword swallowers on the table and footmen behind every chair, but what everyone will remember is the gardenia you floated in their personalized finger bowl. (For a Saturday night event, it's so special to give your guests a copy of Sunday's paper and a boxed breakfast. They'll never forget your kindness.) Barbara and Marvin Davis and their daughter Nancy Davis Rickel have thrown some of the most magnificent parties and charity balls in Beverly Hills. They send you a picture of yourself and your date at the event. What could be better than to remember a great evening with a picture from either the Carousel Ball or the Race to Erase M.S.

FOREIGN AFFAIRS

If you live in a foreign country, always make sure you tell your guests about the currents and the currency. I went grouse shooting in Scotland once and stayed in a magnificent Moorish castle. I brought an adapter for my electric rollers, and when I plugged them in, all the power in the castle went out, maybe even the whole town! But of course, I never admitted to it. I know that, over the years, I've probably blown out the power in a few Caribbean islands too. This is really when you need that small flashlight that you packed.

Make sure you tell your guests the difference between dollars and francs and dollars and pounds or any other currency. If you don't know the currency conversion, use American dollars until you find out the dollar difference. Everyone is always happy to see picture's of our famous Presidents on the bills.

PLANNING THE PERFECT PARTY

Long gone are the days when you grabbed a six-pack, popped some corn, and put on your good underwear. In today's world, a party requires more than a cursory effort on the part of the host. For some people, the very idea of details drives them to distraction and for these individuals, God created the "party planner."

No matter the size of the city you call home, there is either an official party-planning business which will gladly take you as a client, or the unofficial party-planning maven who will gladly do the same. In either case, if you feel at all uneasy about diving into the party arena without a supporting player, feel free to ask for help. A lot can go wrong even with the best of intentions, and it only takes one disaster to taboo you for life.

Theme parties are traditionally the easiest to arrange. They are also likely to turn into total chaos if a little forethought isn't applied.

Nautical themes are all the rage these days. It's a fine choice if you stay on land. Should you feel the urge to go whole hog and charter a yacht, slap yourself silly. Unless it's the *QE2,* the *Sea Goddess,* or the late Malcolm Forbes's *Highlander,* forget it. Too many variables, even if you don't count motion sickness. Guests hate losing the sight of shore for more than a few hours.

The basic rule is that "simpler is better." People don't like to go long distances dressed in absurd costumes, particularly circus costumes. Even though the parties can be fun, people don't like dragging around a 100-pound head of a lion.

If you do decide to throw caution to the wind and opt for a theme event, consider entertaining in a restaurant rather than your home. A Greek party works particularly well, for instance, in a place that is used to making spanikopita and cleaning up broken plates. (The thought of having your Baccarat smashed during the enthusiasm of a Zorba is too much to tolerate. And believe me, it can happen.) The easiest party to do is a color party. Red is always a hit. White for summer. Gold for fall. The theme is endless.

THIS IS YOUR LIFE

By far, the cleverest theme event centers on a guest of honor. Planning your party around a special someone becomes pure inspiration if that someone happens to have enough pull in their own right to attract the perfect guests. Suddenly, the party takes on a life all its own, and you come out looking like the star you are.

HOLIDAY CHEER

The obvious parties—for Christmas and New Year's—are always a hit. The others are for Memorial Day, the Fourth of July, Labor Day, Thanksgiving, and my favorite, Halloween. My friend Clovis Ruffin used to say Halloween was his favorite religious holiday. Whatever the holiday, go for it.

HELLO, IS ANYONE HOME?

The day of the party, make certain that all your guests are telephoned. Remind them that "tonight is the night." It's difficult to believe, but more times than I care to remember, people forget the date of even the most lavish events. Reconfirm your troops. There is nothing more embarrassing than calling the guest of honor the next day asking him why he didn't come to the party, only to be told that he forgot. An ounce of prevention is worth a pound of cure. On two separate occasions when I gave a party Brenda Vaccaro and her husband Guy Hector came a week early!

MUSICAL CHAIRS

The hardest part of party planning to me has always been seating the guests. Every host or hostess has his or her own rules in this area, and custom plays a large role as well. In Europe, it is absolute protocol to split couples up and mix them throughout the party. When this happens to long-marrieds, it usually is a blessing. To young lovers, however, it is a disaster. They spend the entire night pining across the room at one another, making themselves and those around them miserable in the process.

Have Place Card Will Travel

One way to skirt the entire issue is to seat people who arrive together—together. If you feel obligated to split a team, at the very least keep them at the same table where they can keep an eye on one another. Place cards have been used to accomplish this task, though with varying degrees of success. The problem with place cards is that every guest seems to think that he or she knows a *better* way of seating your guests and often times will think nothing of rearranging the cards.

I'll never forget when I gave a party at the famed New York supper club, Le Club. Gossip columnist Cindy Adams called to ask whether the event was "place-carded." At the time, it wasn't an idea that had occurred to me. Grasping the opportunity, I immediately sent out to have place cards printed, and as each person arrived, I handed them their place card and told them to sit where they felt most comfortable. Cindy got a good laugh out of it.

Don't Touch That

You can, of course, obsess on the subject. I had a wonderful friend in New York who was so possessed by the idea that no one should move a place card at any of his events, that at a particular Western-themed party, he placed a lasso through all the place cards and nailed them to the table! It was a clever way of seeing to it that the place card gremlins didn't strike.

The rigidity of place cards has its drawbacks. For one thing, they make it far more difficult to compensate for no-shows. The rule of thumb at parties is that 10 percent of your guests will cancel or 10 percent more than were invited show up. In either case, you must be prepared with your back-up chairs and table. A spare pheasant-under-glass doesn't hurt either.

Another clever way around the seating dilemma is to assign table names which reflect the centerpieces: the rose table, the iris table, the orchid table, etc. Somehow, assigning guests to a "flower" is more personal than merely sending them to table 15. They love it, particularly if you let one lucky guest at each table take home the centerpiece.

Movie themes work well for tables, too. The *Gone with the Wind* table; the *Casablanca* table; the *From Here to Eternity* table. The same goes for famous cities or states. It's wonderful fun.

No matter the seating, it's very important that everyone gets to meet the guest of honor as well as be introduced to one another by the host. Ivana Trump has a wonderful way of handling this. As soon as everyone has been seated, Ivana goes around the room, introducing each person and saying how she knows the person. Since the guest of honor is always seated on her right, she saves that person for last.

Whatever the method, make your introductions and keep things moving. The trick in successful party planning is not to let any element drag out the event. If you have entertainment planned, put it on quickly. People make the mistake of thinking that if they delay the entertainment, everyone will be more excited. In truth, if you hold back the pièce de résistance, they'll be playing to a table of one— yours. The same goes for birthdays. If you have a birthday cake in the wings, the minute they pour the coffee, light the candles. Don't wait.

I'll Drink to That

People would rather meet, mix, and mingle. The best moment of any party is the cocktail hour. But even this part of the event must be kept relatively short or else the more lush among your guests will surely get drunk and unruly. Don't hold your guests prisoner. Begin to time your cocktail hour from the arrival of your first guest. Never drag it out longer than sixty minutes from that point.

The entire meal should never take more than 2 hours. By the time you are serving coffee and dessert, the first-in, first-outers are putting on their wraps, thanking you for the fabulous evening and hitting the road. Do not try to stop them. Welcome the exodus to free up the room so that those who remain can linger over a cup of coffee, an after-dinner drink, a cigar, a joke, and a flirt.

Officially, the party won't break up until after midnight, no matter what the call time. If you're lucky, by twelve-thirty or a quarter to one, you'll be in bed, praying that everyone has gone home. Another tip: Always check the driveway for spare cars before retiring, and don't forget that a house search is not out of the question. There are few things worse than finding a guest passed out when you wake up the next morning, but offhand I can't think of one. When this happens, it's like a bad Broadway play—all melodrama, no applause.

BEST FOOT FORWARD

A final word of advice: Lighten up. Don't ever be afraid to entertain. The worst that can happen is that it will be a fiasco and you'll spend the rest of your natural life cleaning up the pieces. Just kidding! There is little difference between a monumental success and a spectacular flop but most guests don't know the difference. They are so thrilled at being invited.

MUM'S THE WORD

While we're on the subject of contingency plans, never, ever tell the other guests who you expect to attend any of your functions. Reveal the guest list and set yourself up for a fall. If no one knows for certain who else is invited, no one except you will know who doesn't show up. I'm from the school "what they don't know won't hurt them." It also never hurts to have backups ready (i.e., a couple of good friends who don't mind acting as "dress extras" for the evening). In fact, I've got friends that have made something of a career of being fill-ins and are proud of it! They telephone and tell me not to be embarrassed to call at the last minute if I have a drop-out. It's not how they got there; it's *that* they got there.

No Business Like Show Business

Robert Wagner and I gave a party for his beautiful wife, Jill St. John. We had a star-studded guest list that included Barbara and Frank Sinatra, Liza Minelli, and Nancy Kissinger, just to name a few. I never told any of the guests, nor the press, who was invited. When Jill and R.J. (Robert Wagner) picked me up in the limo, they informed me that they didn't think the Sinatra's were coming because their plane hadn't landed yet. I thought to myself, what would have happened if I'd told everyone that they were coming and they didn't show up? It would have been known as the party that the Sinatra's didn't come to instead of the great party for Jill St. John.

Liza Minelli was the first to arrive. And 45 minutes later, the Sinatra's showed up after all. Everyone was in shock, including me. But that goes to prove, mum's the word—never tell who is on your guest list. When my friends call and ask me who's invited to my parties, I tell them, "You'll find out when you get here."

Lights, Camera, Action

In the eighties, I produced and hosted a television program *The Nikki Haskell Show*. Every Friday night, I would throw a party for some famous friend, movie premiere, record launching, or anything else that I thought was amusing. Over the last twenty years, I have bitten off some huge bites in the name of enthusiastic party giving. When Broadway/Hollywood producer Allan Carr premiered the retro film *Where the Boys Are,* I threw a star-studded premiere party at Studio 54 in Manhattan. Since it was a beach movie, I imported 50 tons of white sand and mixed it with flecks of gold; sail boats hanging from the ceiling; muscle men and bathing beauties in bikinis scattered around looking sexy. We brought in ice cream trucks, nautical flags, hot dog wagons, and a few rubber sharks to decorate the bar area. (The real thing would have been too intense even for me.) People are talking about that party to this day.

When I tossed a party for the premiere of the film *Hell's Angels Forever,* we brought in 800 Hell's Angels, who drove their motorcycles from 12th Street up Park Avenue to 57th Street, 57th Street to Seventh

Avenue, and down Seventh Avenue, where we had to block off 54th and Seventh. The highlight of the evening was when I went into the ladies' room and discovered two girls in strapless dresses, completely covered in tattoos. Yes, even I was shocked and it takes a lot to shock me.

On another occasion, I redecorated Studio 54 to look like the set of *The King and I*. Yul Brynner and Michael Jackson were coguests of honor. It's hard to believe that the Gloved One was a close friend of Yul's. When Michael was on tour as a child, he played many of the same towns where Yul was starring in *The King and I*. Over the years, they became the best of friends and remained so until Yul's death.

THRILLER DILLER

No guest of honor was quite as demanding of me as Michael Jackson was. On this particular occasion, his staff called my office and told us that Michael had to have special orange juice from a stand at 84th and Lexington, papaya juice from another stand somewhere in the heart of Chinatown, plus numerous other drinks that had to be brought from other specific places.

Not one to be fooled, when Michael arrived, I had him personally examine the various containers to assure him that he had not been cheated. The highlight of the evening was when Yul Brynner, Michael Jackson, and I went up to the disc jockey booth, where we showed the video of *Thriller* for the first time. The crowd went wild. They didn't know Michael Jackson was coming. Remember: Mum's the word. Which brings me to my next point. Always respect the wishes of your special guests, whether it be food, company, or privacy. Never promise anything you can't deliver.

TROOP CONTROL

Regardless of the size of the events, and no matter how important your guest of honor may be, always keep in mind your responsibility to your other guests. Without them, there would be no party. Individualize your events with your guests in mind, and you'll achieve a much more successful party or weekend. Of course, you'll get the thank-you notes, the flowers, and the telephone calls. But the ultimate pat-on-the-back for all your effort will be an invitation. When it is extended, congratulate yourself. The social ball is rolling.

GUESTS OF GUESTS CANNOT BRING GUESTS—THE DO'S AND DON'TS OF A HOUSEGUEST

I knew that I had died and gone to House Guest Heaven when I was lucky enough to be invited to Arabesque, the winter residence of the Baron and Baroness di Portanova (Ricky and Sandra to their friends.) This spectacular villa located on top of the most beautiful spot in Acapulco, spans the entire side of a mountain and has a breathtaking panoramic view of the Bay of Acapulco. A James Bond movie was at filmed this house. Arabesque is indescribably beautiful—from the hundred white reclining camel statues to the twelve personal-ized guest suites, private pools and beach, water falls, and discotheque. Sandra and Ricky's generosity is world-renowned. Every meal is cooked to perfection and served in the most lavish settings. Frequently, Ricky prepares his famous dishes himself. Every detail of your stay is beyond courteous. I've learned many tips for entertaining from Sandra and Ricky, but the most important is to make your guests feel comfortable and important. And they do just that!

Should you be invited as a houseguest, know that such an honor does not come without its own set of responsibilities. The overriding requirement is to have fun, of course. Sleep late, work on your tan, have lunch, nap, and rejoin the group in time for cocktails, dinner, and watching the sunset.

While doing the above, however, never, ever forget the *Houseguest's Commandments.* This is a list of *do's* and *don'ts* which, if followed, will leave you primed for a wonderful guesting experience. And if you're very lucky, a return invite for next year.

A HOUSEGUEST'S TWENTY COMMANDMENTS

★ **1. Never forget whose bed you're in.** Sleeping with the host or hostess is permitted (if not married), but sleeping with the lover of the host or hostess is not. Or at least, not while you're their guest. Get their number and use it later.

★ **2. Never, ever sleep with the help.** (It does not matter how cute the butler, cook, maid, or chauffeur may be.) This does not mean that you shouldn't befriend the help. Just the opposite. Get to know them immediately.

I know a very famous hostess who was appalled to find out that her chauffer had fathered a child of one of her guests.

★ **3. Never assume that the house is staffed.** Should you be in a home without the luxury of a man-servant, and you can't find a maid to save your life, know that it is *your* responsibility to make your own bed, do your own laundry, and clean your own dishes. In cases such as these, come prepared for a little domestic duty. And never bring a suitcase of dirty laundry expecting that the staff is expected to wash your dirty socks and underwear.

★ **4. Never hire your host's help.** This includes the major domo, chauffeur, cook, or butler. People have been shot for less. That's a definite way to never be invited back again.

★ **5. Never bring anyone home from a party or club.** No matter how tempting. The impact on your reputation may be extraordinary, not to mention that of your host or hostess. On the other hand, if your reputation really needs a little color, bring home anyone you want and get ready for the talk. It will happen.

★ **6. Never give your host's phone number to strangers.** Privacy of your host or hostess is the most important thing that you have to protect. The next thing you know, everybody that they don't want will be calling them to come over. This is the perfect opportunity to bring a portable phone.

★ **7. Never be late for a meal.** There are few things more miserable than a hostess who has to keep the rack of lamb on hold while you finish your nails or trim your sideburns.

★ **8. Never accept outside invitations.** If, as a house guest, you happen to score your own invitation to a fabulous party, share the wealth. Attempt to take your host or hostess with you. The last thing they want to hear is that you've found a bigger name or a better beach.

★ **9. Never ignore your host or hostess.** Always invite them our for lunch or dinner at their convenience. Give a party in their honor. It is a gesture of appreciation.

★ **10. Never bring an entourage.** The cardinal rule is: "Guests of guests cannot bring guests." No one who is a guest dares to bring someone else along without the express permission of your host or hostess. Afterall, it is always the guests of guests who steal the jewelry, drink the liquor, and burn the holes in the duvet cover.

★ **11. Never let it be known you're bored.** The rule here is: Guest, amuse thyself. You should always rent your own car, and bring your own camera and film, tapes, books, pillows, room sprays, sleeping mask, and, soaps, and most of all, medications.

★ **12. Never fail to learn a few key phrases.** If in a foreign country, learn how to ask the following sentences using your cutest accent: "When is breakfast?" "When is lunch?" "When is dinner?" and "Did I receive any calls?" You should be able to order meals in four languages.

★ **13. Never leave a long-distance phone bill behind.** It's totally your responsibility, so use a calling or credit card.

★ **14. Never bring pets, kids, or musical instruments unless specifically included in the invitation.**

★ **15. Never drink all the liquor.** If you're a lush, bring your own booze or send a case to replenish their supply.

★ **16. Never redecorate your room, unless it's your profession.**

★ **17. Never attempt to change the music during lunch or dinner.** For all you know, it could be a *real* string quartet playing Mozart.

★ **18. Never reveal classified information.** What goes on inside the house is no one else's business. I don't care how much the *National Enquirer* or the *Globe* offers you for the story, your lips are sealed.

★ **19. Always tip the help.** Even if your host tells you that it's not necessary, make sure that you definitely tip them. I usually tip them when I get there and when I leave. Then when you return, they will always be thrilled to see you.

★ **20. Never overstay your welcome.** "Fish and houseguests both begin to stink after three days." Know when it's time to leave. If you're supposed to be out by Friday morning at 9 A.M., don't suddenly develop a sore throat that morning at 8:15. Your host may let you stay, but they'll never invite you back.

The Invitation Is in the Mail

Follow the Houseguests Commandments, and I guarantee that you'll be a welcomed return guest in the future. Maintaining an open-door policy with your favorite host or hostess is really as simple as that. It doesn't hurt to stack the odds a little in your favor by bringing a personalized gift when you arrive, plus sending flowers or a note upon returning home. It has also proven helpful to know how to play

tennis or golf; or indoor games such as backgammon, pool, and gin
(A wise guest makes certain the host or hostess wins every so often.)

IS YOUR DANCE CARD FILLED?

Knowing how to dance is another good calling card. When I inter-
viewed Gene Kelly at the Deauville Film Festival, I asked him why
he learned to dance. He said, "The guys who knew how to dance
got all the girls."

Be informative. You must *contribute* to the conversation. Always
try to be an attentive listener. Just keeping an open ear is not enough.
You are expected to have something to talk about (other than business
and yourself) and be able to talk about it cleverly. Always have some
juicy gossip (not about your host), or a funny joke or story to drop
just at the right moment.

It also helps to be beautiful (within bounds), witty (but never
caustic), and smart (but never brilliant). And I must admit that having
a vice or two is extremely helpful in the long run. Nothing is so
ultimately repellant than an individual who is *entirely* good. And once
you return home, it's very important to remember to keep in touch
with your favorite hosts if only to show that you *sincerely* care about
them no matter what the season is.

WHEN THERE'S CAVIAR, ASK FOR CAVIAR

Even the best guests make mistakes. I make them once in a while
myself, and have lived to laugh about them.

It was Valentine's Day, 1977. I was in New York at the time when
I received a called from the Marquis de Portago, who wanted to know
if I could be ready in 15 minutes to fly to Washington for a reception
at the Iranian Embassy. The Iranian Embassy was famous for serving
the finest beluga caviar with magnums of wonderful champagne.
Mention caviar and champagne to me and I can be overdressed and
ready to go in 5 minutes.

We made the flight, checked into a hotel, changed, and arrived at the embassy party late. As we walked in, Andy Warhol was standing at the door. "You guys are late," he told us. "In fact, you're so late, you missed the caviar," he said. I was completely crushed, after having thought of nothing but caviar during the entire flight to Washington.

I scoped out the room and discovered that Andy was right. There was no caviar as far as the eye could see. I cornered a waiter and asked for some caviar. Nothing ventured, nothing gained. The waiter told me that I would have to ask the Ambassador, Ardeshir Zaheydi. He pointed toward a man in a red tie.

Approaching the Ambassador, I introduced myself, said I had arrived late, and asked him if it was possible to have some caviar. The Ambassador could not have been more pleasant. Soon he clapped his hands and directed me to two very large and very accommodating bodyguards. The pair escorted me into an enormous mirror-and-gold-encrusted room with sixty-foot-high domed ceilings with banquettes and tables. Far in the back of the room was Jaime Wyeth, son of famed artist Andrew Wyeth. Also in the group were Truman Capote, *Vogue's* Diana Vreeland, and the designer Halston.

As I sat down and joined their conversation, a butler brought over a massive silver tray heaped with caviar and the assorted fixings. Wyeth's eyes widened in wonderment and asked me if he could have some caviar. Then he said, "Where did you get the caviar?" I answered, "Why?" He said, "They didn't serve caviar." "I asked the Ambassador," came my reply before I had a chance to think of the consequences. "That was clever," he said as he joined in, consuming a caviar-covered toast wedge.

Well, yes—and no. I was clever to the point that I got the caviar. But the inherent risks were great. The Ambassador hadn't put the customary caviar on the table because he hadn't wanted to upstage then-President Jimmy Carter, who that very night was hosting his first State Dinner at the White House. The Ambassador knew that President Carter would serve black-eyed peas and hominy grits. Because the Ambassador was also the ultimate host, he did not want to deny my request. Naturally I apologized profusely. I don't ever remember being so embarrassed.

In the end, I turned into Miss Popularity with a silver tray and beluga caviar, and the next day proved the Ambassador right because

President Carter did serve black-eyed peas and hominy grits. But no one ever heard a word about the caviar served at the Iranian Embassy that night.

THE GRAND FINALE

When people criticize me for my excesses, I gently remind them that unless you risk going too far, you will never, ever know how far you can go. I now pass this knowledge on to you.

As a Star Diet graduate, you have learned how to lose weight, get in shape, and get a grip on life. You've laughed your way through the difficult cravings, stress, and obsessions of everyday living; learned to read a label, identify fat, and know the difference between radicchio and rigatoni; plus discovered the perfect host and hostess in all of us.

While we have shaped up and slimmed down, and trimmed the fat from our diet, the ultimate purpose of all the effort boils down to simply this—feeling good about yourself. Bottom line, it's what we all want.

There is no magic involved here. True happiness is the reward for investing in yourself. If you remember that your dreams are only limited by the effort you're willing to make, you've got the battle half-won. My motto is: "Make every day count and try to get two minutes into every minute."

I started this book by telling you that no one can go on a diet for you. The same thing is true with living life to the fullest. Make the commitment and join me at the party. The best is yet to come.

The Star Diet Calorie Counter And Metric Conversion Charts

With Bob Evans and Faye Dunaway at a party in L.A.

Roger Karnbad

	CALORIES
Abalone, meat only, raw 4 oz	120
Acorn squash: baked, cubed, ½ cup	57
boiled, mashed, ½ cup	41
Almond: dried, dry-roasted or toasted	167
oil-roasted, 1 oz, approx 22 kernels	176
Anchovy, canned in olive oil, drained, 5 medium or .7 oz	42
Apple: peeled, sliced, ½ cup	31
unpeeled, 1 medium, 3 per lb	81
Apple juice, canned or bottled, 6 fl oz	87
Applesauce, canned sweetened, ½ cup	97
unsweetened, ½ cup	53
Apricot: canned, in heavy syrup, unpeeled halves, ½ cup	107
canned, in juice halves, ½ cup	60
halves, ½ cup	37
3 medium, 4 oz or 12 per lb	51
Apricot nectar, canned, 6 fl oz	106
Artichoke: boiled, drained, hearts, ½ cup	42
boiled, drained, 1 medium or 10.6 oz	25
frozen, hearts, boiled, drained, 4 oz	51
Arugula, fresh, 2 oz	5
Asparagus, boiled, drained, 4 spears, ½ "-diameter base	15
Avocado: California, 1 medium or 8 oz	306
California, pureed, ½ cup	204
Bacon, cooked, 3 slices, 20 slices per lb	109
Bacon, Canadian style, grilled, 2 medium slices	86
Bacon bits, imitation, 1 tsp	12

Bagel, plain or egg, 2-oz piece	150
Baked beans, canned, plain or vegetarian, ½ cup	118
Beef: (4 oz) round, eye of, roasted, lean only	198
round, top, broiled, lean only	214
shortrib, braised, lean with separable fat	534
sirloin, top, broiled, lean only	229
T-bone steak, broiled, lean, with separable fat	338
tenderloin, broiled, lean with separable fat	345
tenderloin, broiled, lean only	252
Beef, corned, brisket, cured, cooked, 4 oz	285
Beef, corned, hash, canned, 4 oz	200
Beef, dried, cured, 1 oz	47
Beer: regular, 4.5% alcohol, 1 fl oz	12
light, 4% alcohol, 1 fl oz	8
Beets: boiled, drained, sliced, ½ cup	26
canned, Harvard, with liquid, sliced, ½ cup	89
Beet greens, boiled, drained, 1" pieces, ½ cup	20
Black beans, boiled, ½ cup	113
Blackberries, trimmed, ½ cup	37
Blueberries, trimmed, ½ cup	41
Bluefish, meat only, raw, 4 oz	140
Bologna, 1 oz	70
Bouillon cubes:1 cube	8
Bread, commercial: cinnamon raisin, 1 slice	65
french, 1-oz slice	75
granola or multigrain, 1 slice	65
Italian, 1-oz slice	70
oat bran, 1 slice	70
oatmeal, 1 slice	85
pita, 1 piece	150
raisin with cinnamon, 1-oz slice	70
rye or pumpernickel, 1 slice	70
sourdough, French, 1 slice	75
wheat, cracked, 1 slice	65
wheat, whole, 1 slice	70
white, 1 slice	75
white, thin-sliced, 1 slice	50
Bread crumbs, dry, grated, 1tbsp	22
Breadstick, regular, 1 stick, 4½ " long	38
Broccoli: boiled, drained, chopped, ½ cup	22
raw, chopped, ½ cup	12

Brussels sprouts: boiled, drained, 1 sprout, .7 oz	8
frozen, boiled, drained, ½ cup	33
Butter, salted or unsalted: regular, 1 tbsp	100
whipped, 1 tbsp	67
whipped, 1 tsp	23
Butternut squash: baked, cubed, ½ cup	41
frozen, boiled, drained, mashed, ½ cup	47
Cabbage: raw, shredded, ½ cup	8
boiled, drained, shredded, ½ cup	16
Chinese (bok choy), raw, trimmed, 4 oz	16
red, raw, shredded, ½ cup	10
Candy, 1 oz, expect as noted: almonds, candy coated	120
Baby Ruth	130
bridge mix	130
butterscotch	115
caramel	110
cherry, chocolate coated	110
chocolate, milk or dark	150
chocolate, milk, with almonds	157
chocolate, milk, candy coated (M&M's)	250
chocolate, milk, with fruit and nuts	150
coconut, chocolate coated	140
fudge	120
gum, chewing, 1 average stick	10
gum drops, jelled or gummey candy	100
hard candy	110
licorice, candy coated	106
Mars, 1.76-oz bar	240
marshmallow	100
Milky Way	280
mints	110
mints, chocolate coated	120
peanut brittle	130
peanuts, chocolate coated	150
popcorn, caramel coated, with peanuts	120
raisins, chocolate coated	130
taffy	110
toffee	130
Cantaloupe: ½ of 5" diameter melon	94
cubed, ½ cup	29
Carrot: boiled, drained, sliced, ½ cup	35

raw, 1 medium, 7½ " long, 2.8 oz	31
Carrot juice, canned or bottled, 6 fl oz	73
Cashew, 1 oz, approx 18 kernels	163
Catsup, 1 tbsp	16
Cauliflower: frozen boiled, drained, 1" pieces, ½ cup	15
raw, 3 flowerets, approx 5 oz	13
Caviar, granular, black or red, 1 tbsp	40
Celery, raw: 1 stalk, 7½ " long, approx 1.6 oz	6
diced, ½ cup	10
Cereal, ready to eat, dry, 1 oz:	
bran flakes	90
bran flakes with raisins	100
corn, toasted or flakes	110
granola	130
mixed grains	110
oats or oat bran	110
rice, crisped or puffed	110
Chayote, raw, 1" pieces, ½ cup	16
Cheese, 1 oz, except as noted:	
American or pimiento, processed	106
blue	100
brick	105
Brie	95
Camembert	85
cheddar	114
colby	112
cottage cheese, creamed	29
cottage cheese, low-fat, 1%	20
cream cheese	99
Edam or Gouda	101
farmer	100
feta, sheep's milk	75
fontina	110
gjetost, goat's milk	132
Jarlsberg	100
Limburger	93
Monterrey Jack	106
mozzarella, whole milk	80
mozzarella, whole milk, low-moisture	90
Muenster	104
Parmesan, hard	111

Parmesan, grated, 1 tbsp	23
Port du Salut	100
provolone	100
ricotta, whole milk	49
ricotta, part-skim milk	39
Romano	110
Roquefort, sheeps milk	105
string	80
Swiss, natural	107
Swiss, processed	95
Tilsit, whole milk	96
Cherries: sour, red, ½ cup	39
sweet, ½ cup	52
Chicken: broiler or fryer, fried, flour coated, meat with skin: breast, 4 oz	252
dark meat, 4 oz	323
skin only, 1 oz	142
wings, 4 oz	364
broiler or roaster: roasted dark meat only 4 oz	232
light meat only, 4 oz	196
skin only, 1 oz	129
capon, roasted, meat with skin, 4 oz	260
Clam juice bottled, 3 fl oz	4
Cocoa mix, powder, 1 oz or 3–4 heaping tsp	102
Coconut, shelled: 1 piece, 2" x 2" x ½ ", 1.6 oz	159
dried, sweetened, flaked, packaged, 1 oz	134
Cod, meat only: baked, broiled, or microwaved, 4 oz	119
canned, with liquid, 4 oz	119
dried, salted, 1 oz	81
raw, 4 oz	93
Coffee, brewed, 6 fl oz	4
Collards: boiled, drained, chopped, ½ cup	17
raw, chopped, ½ cup	6
Cookies: brownie, from mix, with nuts, 1 oz	114
butter flavor, 1 oz	130
chocolate, 1 oz	126
chocolate chip, 1 oz	134
chocolate snaps or wafers (Nabisco), ½ oz	70
coconut bar, 1 oz	140
cream sandwich, chocolate (Oreo), ½-oz piece	50
fig bar (fig Newtons), ½-oz piece	60

gingersnaps, 1 oz	119
graham cracker, chocolate coated, 2" x 2 ½ " piece	62
graham cracker, plain, 5" x 2 ½ " piece	55
graham cracker, sugar honey, 5 ½ " x 2 ½ " piece	58
ladyfinger, 1 oz	102
macaroon, 1 oz	135
marshmallow, chocolate cake (Mallomars), ½-oz piece	60
molasses, 1 oz	120
oatmeal with raisins, 1 oz	123
peanut, sandwich or sugar wafers, 1 oz	134
peanut butter, 1 oz	150
raisin, biscuit type, 1 oz	107
shortbread (Lorna Doone), 3 pieces or ½ oz	70
shortbread, pecan (Pecan Sandies), ½-oz piece	80
sugar wafer (Biscos), 4 pieces or ½ oz	70
tea biscuit (Social Tea), ⅙-oz piece	20
vanilla wafer, 1 oz	131
Corn: canned, kernels, drained, ½ cup	66
kernels, boiled, drained, ½ cup	89
Cornbread, mix, prepared with milk and egg, 2 ½ " square	178
Corn chips or puffs, regular or tortilla, 1 oz	145
Cornmeal, degermed, ½ cup	253
Crab, meat only: Alaska king, boiled, poached, or steamed, 4 oz	110
blue, boiled, poached, or steamed, 4 oz	116
dungeness, raw, 4 oz	97
Crackers: arrowroot biscuit (National), ¼-oz piece	20
cheese or cheese flavor, 1 oz	136
cheese sandwich, ½-oz piece	70
matzo, 1-oz board	115
melba toast, plain or seasoned, 1 oz	105
Pepperidge Farm Original Goldfish, 1 oz	130
rye, seasoned (Ry-Krisp), ½ oz	45
saltine, 1 oz	123
saltine (Premium), 5 pieces	60
sesame bread wafer (Meal Mates), 3 pieces or ½ oz	70
soda or water, 1 oz	124
soup and oyster (oysterettes), 18 pieces or ½ oz	60
wheat (Triscuit), 3 pieces or ½ oz	60
wheat, whole, 1 oz	114
Zwieback toast (Nabisco), 2 pieces or ½ oz	60
Cranberry juice cocktail, bottled, 6 fl oz	108

Cranberry-orange relish, canned, ¼ cup	123
Cream, fluid half and half, 1 tbsp	20
light, coffee or table, 1 tbsp	29
whipping, heavy, 1 tbsp (2 tbsp whipped)	52
Cream, sour, 1 oz	26
Croissant, butter, 2-oz piece	200
Crookneck squash: boiled, drained, sliced, ½ cup	18
frozen, boiled, drained, sliced, ½ cup	24
Croutons, seasoned, ½ oz	65
Cucumber, unpeeled:	
1 medium, 8¼ " long, 10.9 oz	39
sliced, ½ cup	7
Currants: black, trimmed, ½ cup	36
red or white, trimmed, ½ cup	31
Dates, domestic, natural and dry, 10 dates or 2.9 oz	228
Duck, domesticated, roasted: meat with skin, 4 oz	382
meat only, 4 oz	228
Egg, chicken, fresh: raw, whole, 1 large egg, approximately 1.75 oz	75
raw, white from 1 large egg	17
raw, yolk from 1 large egg (with small portion of white)	59
Eggnog, nonalcoholic, chilled, 1 cup	342
Eggplant, boiled, drained, 1" cubes, ½ cup	13
Falafel, 1 patty, 2¼ " diameter	57
Figs: 1 medium, 1.8 oz	37
canned in light syrup, 3 figs and 1¾ tbsp syrup	58
Filberts, shelled, 1 oz	179
Fish fillets, frozen, breaded, reheated, 2-oz piece	155
Frankfurter, beef, 2-oz link, 5" long × ⅞"	184
Fruit, mixed: canned, fruit salad, in juice, ½ cup	62
canned in heavy syrup, ½ cup	92
dried, pitted, 1 oz	69
Fruit punch juice drink, frozen, diluted, 8 fl oz	123
Gelatin, unflavored, dry, 1 tbsp	33
Gelatin dessert mix, flavored, prepared, ½ cup	80
Goose, domesticated: roasted, meat only, 4 oz	270
roasted, meat with skin, 4 oz	346
Grape: slipskin (Concord, Delaware, etc.), untrimmed, 1 lb	165
slipskin, peeled and seeded, ½ cup	29
Grape juice, canned or bottled, 6 fl oz	116
Grapefruit: canned in juice, ½ cup	46
pink and red, ½ of 3 ¾ "-diameter fruit, 8.5 oz	37

Grapefruit juice: canned or bottled, 6 fl oz	70
fresh, 6 fl oz	72
Great northern beans: canned with liquid, ½ cup	150
dried, boiled, ½ cup	104
Green beans, whole or cut, boiled, drained, ½ cup	22
Grouper, mixed species, meat only, baked, broiled, or microwaved, 4 oz	134
Guava, 1 medium, approx 4 oz	45
Halibut, Atlantic and Pacific, meat only, baked, broiled, or microwaved, 4 oz	159
Ham, boneless, roasted: fresh, rump, separable lean and fat, 4 oz	311
fresh, rump, separable lean only, 4 oz	251
Ham salad spread, 1 tbsp	32
Herring, Atlantic, meat only: kippered, 4 oz	246
pickled, 4 oz	297
Honey, 1 tbsp	64
Honeydew: ⅒ of 7"-diameter melon, 2" slice, 8 oz	46
cubed, ½ cup	30
Hubbard squash: baked, cubed, ½ cup	51
boiled, drained, mashed, ½ cup	35
Hummus, 1 tbsp	26
Ice cream, vanilla: regular, 10% fat, hardened, ½ cup	134
rich, 16% fat, hardened, ½ cup	175
soft-serve (frozen custard), ½ cup	189
Ice cream bar, chocolate coated, 3 fl oz bar	162
Ice cream cone, plain (unfilled): sugar, 1 piece	37
waffle, 1 piece	19
Ice milk, vanilla, hardened, ½ cup	92
Ices, water, flavored, ½ cup	124
Jam and preserves, all flavors, 1 tbsp	54
Jerusalem artichoke, sliced, ½ cup	57
Kale: boiled, drained, chopped, ½ cup	21
raw, trimmed, 1 oz	14
Kidney beans, red, all varieties: boiled, ½ cup	112
canned, with liquid, ½ cup	104
Kiwi fruit, 1 medium, approx 3 oz	46
Knockwurst, pork and beef, 1 oz	87
Kohlrabi: boiled, drained, sliced, ½ cup	24
raw, sliced, ½ cup	19
Lamb, domestic, choice grade, 4 oz: leg, sirloin, roasted, separable lean and fat	331

leg, sirloin, roasted, separable lean only	231
leg and shoulder, cubed for stew, braised	253
Leeks, trimmed: boiled, drained, I medium, 4.4 oz	38
boiled, drained, chopped, ½ cup	16
Lemonade, frozen, diluted, 8 fl oz	100
Lemon juice, I tbsp	4
Lentils, boiled, ½ cup	115
Lettuce: iceberg, 6"-diameter head, 1.25 lb	70
iceberg, I leaf, .7 oz	3
looseleaf, trimmed, I oz or ½ cup shredded	5
Lima beans: boiled, drained, ½ cup	104
frozen, baby, boiled, drained, ½ cup	94
frozen, fordhook, boiled, drained, ½ cup	85
Limeade, frozen, diluted, 8 fl oz	102
Lime juice, I tbsp	4
Liquor, pure distilled (bourbon, gin, rye, vodka, etc.): 80 proof, I fl oz	65
90 proof, I fl oz	74
100 proof, I fl oz	83
Liver: beef, pan-fried, 4 oz	246
chicken, simmered, 4 oz	178
Lobster, northern, meat only: boiled, poached, or steamed, 4 oz	111
raw, 4 oz	104
Lychee: dried, I oz	79
raw, shelled and seeded, I oz	19
Macadamia nut, shelled: oil-roasted, I oz, 10–12 whole kernels	204
Macaroni (see also Pasta): cooked, elbows, I cup	197
cooked, vegetable, rainbow, or tricolor, 4 oz	145
Mango: I medium, 10.6 oz	135
sliced, ½ cup	54
Maple syrup, I tbsp	50
Margarine, regular, I tbsp	100
Mayonnaise: I tbsp	100
reduced-calorie, I tbsp	50
Melon balls, cantaloupe and honeydew, frozen, ½ cup	28
Milk, cow, fluid: buttermilk, cultured, I cup	99
evaporated, skim, ½ cup	100
low-fat, 1% fat, I cup	102
low-fat, 2% fat, I cup	121
skim, I cup	86
whole, 3.3% fat, I cup	150

Molasses: blackstrap, 1 tbsp	43
light, 1 tbsp	50
Monkfish, meat only, raw, 4 oz	87
Muffins: blueberry or corn, 2-oz piece	175
English (Pepperidge Farm), 1 piece	140
Mushroom: raw, 1 medium, .7 oz	5
raw, pieces, ½ cup	9
canned, drained, pieces, ½ cup	19
Mushroom, **Shiitake,** dried, 4 medium or ½ oz	44
Mussels, blue, meat only, boiled or steamed, 4 oz	195
Mustard, prepared: Dijon, 1 tsp	8
yellow, 1 tsp	4
Mustard greens: raw, trimmed, 1 oz or ½ cup chopped	7
boiled, drained, chopped, ½ cup	11
Navy beans, dried, boiled, ½ cup	129
Nectarine, 1 medium, 2 ½ " diameter, 5.3 oz	67
Noodles: Chinese, cellophane or long rice, dehydrated, 2 oz	199
egg, cooked, 1 cup	212
chow mein, 1 cup, approximately 1.5 oz	237
Oat bran, dry, ¼ cup or .8 oz	58
Oats, rolled or oatmeal, cooked, 1 cup	145
Oil, vegetable, nut, or seed, all varieties, 1 tbsp	120
Okra, boiled, drained, sliced, ½ cup	25
Olive, pickled, green, pitted, 1 oz	33
Onion, green (scallion), trimmed, with top, chopped, ¼ cup	8
Onion, mature, raw, chopped, ¼ cup	60
Onion rings, breaded, frozen, oven-heated, 2 rings, 7 oz	81
Orange: California navel, 1 medium, 7.3 oz	65
Florida, sections without membrane, ½ cup	42
Orange juice, fresh or chilled, 6 fl oz	83
Oysters, Eastern, meat only: boiled, poached or steamed, 4 oz	155
raw, 1 cup	170
raw, 6 medium, approximately 3 oz or 70 per quart	58
Pancake and waffle mix, prepared, plain or buttermilk, 4"-diameter cake	61
Papaya, whole, 1 medium or 1 lb	117
Parsnip, boiled, drained, sliced, ½ cup	63
Passion fruit, purple, 1 medium, 1.2 oz	18
Pasta, dry, plain, cooked, all varieties, 1 cup	197
Pastrami, beef, 1 oz	99

Pâté, canned:

chicken liver, 1 tbsp	26
goose liver, smoked, 1 tbsp	60
Peach: canned in light syrup, halves or slices, ½ cup	68
1 medium, 2 ½ " diameter, 4 per lb	37
peeled, sliced, ½ cup	37
Peach nectar, canned or bottled, 6 fl oz	101
Peanut butter, chunk or smooth style, 2 tbsp	188
Pear: Bartlett, 2 ½ " diameter, approx 2 ½ per lb	98
canned in juice, halves, ½ cup	62
Pear nectar, canned, 6 fl oz	112
Peas; edible-podded, boiled, drained, ½ cup	34
green or sweet, boiled, drained, ½ cup	67
Pecans, shelled:	
dried, 1 oz	190
dry-roasted, 1 oz	187
oil-roasted, 1 oz	195
Pepper, chili, hot, red and green: canned, with liquid, chopped, ½ cup	17
raw, 1 medium, 1.6 oz	18
Pepper, jalapeño, canned or in jars, with liquid, ½ cup	17
Pepper, sweet, green and red: boiled, drained, chopped, ½ cup	19
raw, 1 medium, approx 3.2 oz	20
Perch, mixed species, meat only, baked, broiled, or microwaved, 4 oz	133
Persimmon, native, fresh, 1 medium, 1.1 oz	32
Pickle: bread and butter, 1 oz	21
dill, 1 oz	5
sweet, 1 large, 3" long, 1.2 oz	41
Pie, frozen, baked: apple, ⅙ of 8" pie	231
cherry, ⅙ of 8" pie	282
Pine nuts pignolia, dried, shelled, 1 oz	146
Pineapple: canned in juice, cut or crushed, ½ cup	70
fresh, sliced, 3-oz slice, 3 ½ " diameter	42
Pineapple juice, canned or bottled, 6 fl oz	104
Pistachio nuts: dried, shelled, 1 oz, approx 47 kernels	164
dry-roasted, shelled, 1 oz	172
Pizza, cheese, frozen, 10" diameter pie	973
Plum, pitted, sliced, ½ cup	46
Pomegranate, 1 medium, 9.7 oz	104

Popcorn, popped, plain, I cup, approx .8 oz	23
Pork, fresh (see also Ham): loin, center, roasted, separable lean and fat, 4 oz	346
loin, center, roasted, separable lean only, 4 oz	272
Potato (see also Sweet potato) baked in skin, I medium, approx 7 oz	220
baked in skin, pulp only, ½ cup, 2.2 oz	57
boiled without skin, I medium, 2 ½ " diameter, 4.8 oz	116
mashed, with whole milk, ½ cup	81
mashed, with whole milk and butter, ½ cup	111
Pretzels, I oz	111
Prosciutto, I oz	90
Prune, dried, pitted, uncooked, 10 medium or 3 oz	201
Prune juice, canned or bottled, 6 fl oz	136
Pudding mix, regular, prepared with whole milk, ½ cup	165
Radish, raw, 10 medium, 1.8 oz	7
Raisins, seedless, I oz	85
Raspberries, trimmed, ½ cup	31
Refried beans, canned, ½ cup	134
Relish, pickle, sweet, I tbsp	21
Rhubarb, unsweetened, raw, diced, ½ cup	13
Rice, cooked (see also Wild rice):	
brown, long grain, ½ cup	108
white, long grain, parboiled, ½ cup	100
Rolls: dinner or pan, I-oz piece	83
hamburger or hot dog, 1.4-oz piece	119
hard, round or kaiser, 3 ½ " diameter, 1-¾ oz	156
Roughy, **orange,** meat only, raw, 4 oz	80
Rutabaga, boiled, drained, cubed, ½ cup	29
Salad dressing, bottled, I tbsp	65
Salami: beef and pork, cooked, I oz	71
dry or hard, pork and beef, I oz	119
Salmon, meat only: Atlantic, raw, 4 oz	160
Chinook, raw, 4 oz	204
Chinook, smoked, regular or lox, 4 oz	133
Sardines, canned in oil, Atlantic, drained, 2 oz	118
Sauerkraut, canned with liquid, ½ cup	22
Sausage (see also Frankfurter, and specific listings): pork, cooked, I patty, I oz yield from 2 oz raw	100
Scallops, mixed species, meat only, raw, 2 large or 5 small, 1.1 oz	26
Sesame seeds, dried, whole, I oz	162

Shallots, raw, chopped, 1 tbsp	7
Shark, mixed species, meat only, raw, 4 oz	148
Sherbet, orange, ½ cup	135
Shortening, household, 1 tbsp	115
Shrimp, mixed species, meat only: boiled, poached, or steamed, 4 oz	112
canned, drained, 1 cup or 4.5 oz	154
raw, 4 large or 1 oz	30
Snapper, mixed species, meat only: baked, broiled, or microwaved, 4 oz	145
raw, 4 oz	112
Soda and soft drinks, 8 fl oz: club soda or seltzer	0
cola	96
cream soda	105
fruit-flavored	113
ginger ale	76
root beer	100
tonic or quinine water	76
Soup, canned, ready-to-serve, 1 cup: bean with ham, chunky	231
beef, chunky	171
beef broth or bouillon	16
borscht	100
chicken noodle	99
chicken rice, chunky	127
chicken vegetable, chunky	167
clam chowder, Manhattan, chunky	133
escarole	27
gazpacho	57
Lentil with ham	140
Spinach: boiled, drained, ½ cup	21
raw, trimmed, 1 oz or ½ cup chopped	6
Split peas, boiled, ½ cup	116
Squid, mixed species, meat only: dried, 1 oz	86
raw, 4 oz	104
Strawberries, trimmed, ½ cup	23
Succotash, boiled, drained, ½ cup	111
Sugar, beet or cane: brown, ½ cup, not packed	271
granulated, 1 tsp	15
granulated, ½ cup	385
Sweet and sour sauce, Chinese style, 1 tbsp	30
Sweet potato, baked in skin, 1 potato, 5" x 2", 5.1 oz	118

Swiss chard: boiled, drained, chopped, ½ cup	18
raw, chopped, ½ cup	3
Swordfish, meat only: baked, broiled, or microwaved, 4 oz	176
raw, 4 oz	137
Tangerine: mandarin orange, canned in juice, ½ cup	46
I medium, 2 ⅜ " diameter, 4.1 oz	37
Tartar sauce, I tbsp	74
Tea, brewed, 6 fl oz	2
Tempeh, ½ cup or 3 oz	165
Teriyaki sauce, I tbsp	15
Tofu: raw, firm, I oz	41
salted and fermented (fuyu), I oz	33
Tomato, red, ripe: canned, whole, 4 oz, approx ½ cup	23
canned, stewed, ½ cup	34
raw, 2⅗" diameter, 4.75 oz	26
raw, chopped, ½ cup	19
Tomato juice, canned or bottled, 6 fl oz	32
Tomato sauce, canned, ½ cup	37
Trout, meat only, 4 oz: mixed species, raw	168
rainbow, raw	133
rainbow, baked, broiled, or microwaved	171
Tuna, meat only: bluefin, raw, 4 oz	164
canned, light, in oil, drained, 2 oz	112
canned, light, in water, drained, 2 oz	74
Turkey, boneless and luncheon meat, cooked, breast, I oz	31
Turkey, fresh, roasted, 4 oz: meat only	193
dark meat only	212
light meat only	178
Turkey bologna, I oz	57
Turnip, boiled, drained, cubed, ½ cup	14
Turnip greens, boiled, drained, chopped, ½ cup	15
Veal, meat only, 4 oz: cubed for stew, braised, separable lean only	213
ground, boiled	195
loin, roasted, separable lean and fat	246
loin, roasted, separable lean only	198
Vegetable juice cocktail, canned, 6 fl oz	34
Venison, meat only, roasted, 4 oz	179
Vinegar, cider or distilled, I tbsp	2
Walnuts, dried, English or Persian, shelled, I oz	182
Waterchestnuts, Chinese, sliced, ½ cup	66
Watercress, chopped, ½ cup	2

Watermelon, diced, ½ cup	25
Wheat germ, toasted, 1 oz, approx ¼ cup	108
White beans, boiled, ½ cup	125
Worcestershire sauce (Lea & Perrins), 1 tsp	5
Yam, *see* Sweet potato	
Yellow squash, *see* Crookneck squash	
Yogurt, plain: low-fat, 8 oz	139
skim milk, 8 oz	127
whole milk, 8 oz	144
Zucchini: boiled, drained, sliced, ½ cup	14
raw, sliced, ½ cup	9

APPENDIX II

How to Create Your Own Star Diet Diary

With Beverly Johnson and Christopher Lambert

The Star Diet Diary is one of the most important tools you will use in your attempt to lose weight. Write down *everything* you eat and drink every day.

1. Begin with the first thing you eat in the morning up to the last morsel of food and/or liquids that you put in your mouth before you go to sleep. Record the time that you eat and the amount of your food and beverage intake. Also, include things added to food such as butter, mayonnaise, cream, ketchup, etc.

2. Record all food and list their correct calorie count using the Star Diet Calorie Counter included in this book. If the item is not included in the Calorie Counter, check the calories on the Nutrition Facts label on the package.

3. Add up the calories for each item . . . all items for breakfast, lunch, dinner, and snacks, including beverages. And put in the total for every meal. Be sure to make a total count at the end of the day.

4. List all your liquid intake. This will include water, coffee, tea, soft drinks, and liquor.

5. At the bottom, note all social events, parties, birthdays, etc. This is when you find that you most fall off the diet wagon. Also, note here if you are feeling depressed, lonely, sad, or upset that day. You may notice a pattern of eating related to your mood.

6. Be complete and honest. I know that it is easy to forget those

little M&M's, potato chips, and other snacks that you are trying to avoid. Even if you eat something off somebody else's plate, make sure that you record it as every morsel of food and every beverage counts. Just remember, *Honesty is the key to success.*

7. Describe your exercise program for each day, whether it is aerobics, walking, or dancing. Describe in detail each activity and the level of exercise. If you engage in a sport such as golf, tennis, swimming, basketball, or even butterfly catching, make a note in your diary.

8. The accuracy of your diary will give you an overview of where your strong and weak points are and allow you to plan ahead. That way you will have a broad view of which meals are easier for you than others and when you have your most food intake.

9. And if you have a bad day, don't give up. Make sure that you start the next day all over again.

10. Carry this diet diary with you and record as you eat. Otherwise you may forget. And if you cannot bring this diary with you every day, make sure you write what you eat on a piece of paper and transfer it to your diary at the end of the day. This is your most important document, and it will help you lose weight easier and faster. We have given you a one-week diary. Be sure to make copies for longer periods. You will find that, in your battle for weight loss, it will become easier as you go along.

STAR DIET DIARY

DAY ONE

Date:		Weight:	
Time	FOOD AND AMOUNTS		Calories
	Breakfast *"drink a cup of warm water and lemon"*		
	Lunch		
	Dinner		
	Snack		
	Liquids		
	Exercise		
		Total Daily Calories	
Notes:			

STAR DIET DIARY

DAY TWO

Date:		Weight:	
Time	FOOD AND AMOUNTS		Calories
	Breakfast *"drink a cup of warm water and lemon"*		
	Lunch		
	Dinner		
	Snack		
	Liquids		
	Exercise		
		Total Daily Calories	
Notes:			

STAR DIET DIARY

DAY THREE

Date:		Weight:	
Time	FOOD AND AMOUNTS		Calories
	Breakfast *"drink a cup of warm water and lemon"*		
	Lunch		
	Dinner		
	Snack		
	Liquids		
	Exercise		
		Total Daily Calories	
Notes:			

STAR DIET DIARY

DAY FOUR

Date:		Weight:	
Time	FOOD AND AMOUNTS		Calories
	Breakfast *"drink a cup of warm water and lemon"*		
	Lunch		
	Dinner		
	Snack		
	Liquids		
	Exercise		
		Total Daily Calories	
Notes:			

STAR DIET DIARY

DAY FIVE

Date:		Weight:	
Time	FOOD AND AMOUNTS		Calories
	Breakfast *"drink a cup of warm water and lemon"*		
	Lunch		
	Dinner		
	Snack		
	Liquids		
	Exercise		
		Total Daily Calories	
Notes:			

STAR DIET DIARY

DAY SIX

Date:		Weight:	
Time	FOOD AND AMOUNTS		Calories
	Breakfast *"drink a cup of warm water and lemon"*		
	Lunch		
	Dinner		
	Snack		
	Liquids		
	Exercise		
	Total Daily Calories		
Notes:			

STAR DIET DIARY

DAY SEVEN

Date:		Weight:	
Time	FOOD AND AMOUNTS		Calories
	Breakfast *"drink a cup of warm water and lemon"*		
	Lunch		
	Dinner		
	Snack		
	Liquids		
	Exercise		
		Total Daily Calories	
Notes:			

A Fun Glossary of Foods Your Mother Never Told You About

With Claude Montana and Cher at the Cannes film festival.

Everyone knows what it's like to sit down at a restaurant and open the menu, only to find it's written in French or Italian. Perhaps you've found yourself in the ethnic or gourmet aisle at the supermarket wondering what all those exotic foodstuffs were. Unless you speak the language, bring an interpreter, or are especially fortunate in your dinner companion, you'll find yourself either pointing to something unpronounceable or embarrassing yourself by ordering in your high school French. It's even more embarrassing to sit down at a restaurant in West Los Angeles and open an English menu, only to find that you don't know how to order in your native tongue. *What is all this stuff?* you wonder, and consider ordering a chicken salad in hopes that something on the menu fits this description. Since *haute cuisine* has found its way into frozen dinners and family restaurants in America's heartland, more and more diners are sitting down and wondering what to order among the baffling new array of choices. Just so you don't have to eat chicken salad for the rest of your life, let me introduce you to some of the more exotic ingredients gracing today's menus. Not all of them are recommended for Star Dieters, but at least you'll know what you're ordering if you do decide to indulge.

I've prepared the following Glossary of Foods Your Mother Never Told You About so that you'll be a savvy Star Diner and broaden your food horizons.

GLOSSARY

A

abbacchio [ah-BAHK-ee-yoh] Young lamb in Italian. Not to be confused with AGNEAU.

agneau [an-YOH] A mature lamb, according to the French.

aigre-doux [ay-greh-DOO] If you've ever eaten Chinese sweet-and-sour sauce, you get the point here.

aïoli [ay-OH-lee] A type of mayonnaise almost as heavy in fat as it is in garlic. Served with meats, fish, and vegetables in French restaurants.

aji-no-moto [ah-JEE-no-MO-toh] The Japanese knock off of monosodium glutamate (MSG), and just as bad for you as the original.

akala [ah-KALH-ah] A large, overripe, Hawaiian fruit which resembles the raspberry, but tastes sweeter and has far more juice.

akule [ah-KOO-lay] A Hawaiian word for the Bigeye Scad fish.

Albert sauce The ingredients are horseradish, cream, flour, and butter, and you'll find it spooned over beef. Star Dieters immediately spoon it off.

albondiga [al-BON-dee-gah] A meatball by any other name. In this case, a Mexican meatball usually served in a spicy tomato sauce.

alewife [ale-wife] Don't expect a drunken homemaker. Order alewife and get herring.

allumettes [al-yoo-MEHT] The tiniest French fries in existence. Good, fattening, and off-limits.

amandine [AH-mon-deen] The French version of slivered almonds. If you see it on a menu misspelled "almondine," leave immediately. You've made the wrong reservation.

anchovy [ANN-cho-vey]   More than the things you never order on pizza and remove from your Caesar Salad, anchovies are an assortment of small, silver fish which when filleted and oiled turn into a highly salty, a-little-goes-a-long-way garnish.

andouille sausage [an-DWEE]   You'll find this no-no in Cajun cooking. Before tasting, know that this sausage contains tripe and chitterlings (the small intestines of pigs). Yum. Fattening too.

angel hair pasta   The thinnest pasta known to man or beast. Also called *capelli d'angelo*. Delicious in any language. A treat for Star Dieters since it is usually accompanied by a light sauce, and the pasta itself is low-calorie and delicious.

angels on horseback   No winged jockeys but rather oysters wrapped in bacon and served on buttered toast points. Let them fly by.

antipasto [an-tee-PAST-oh]   In Italian, this literally means "before the pasta." In America, it's usually a fancy way to say appetizer. A variety of meats, cheeses, olives, and marinated vegetables. Beware the restaurant that lists a small pasta dish as an "antipasto." Only in New York would they think this is cute.

arugula [ah-ROO-gu-la]   The fancy name for a green served in many Italian restaurants. Arugula looks like radish leaves and tastes just as bitter.

au bleu [oh-BLUH]   Leave it to the French to think up such a romantic-sounding phrase. You'll find it on the menu attached to a fish which has been quickly killed and plunged into a pot of simmering bouillon broth. Its skin turns blue—at the very least.

avgolemono [ahv-go-LEH-moh-noh]   This mouthful is the Greek way of telling you that you're getting a soup made of chicken broth, lemon juice, and egg yolks with rice.

B

b'steeya [bs-TEE-yah]   A favorite of the late Malcolm Forbes, this dish is from Morocco. Phyllo dough is layered with by shredded pigeon and ground almonds. The concoction is then baked and sprinkled with powdered sugar.

baba ghanoush [ba-bah ga-NOOSH] Puree eggplant, garlic, lemon juice, and olive oil with TAHINI, then top with pomegranate seeds or pistachio nuts. Baba ghanoush is a lower-cal dip that's a hit with PITA bread.

baguette [ba-GET] The long, narrow French bread that has popped up in supermarkets slipped into white paper bags. Rather fancy until you realize that in France it's table bread for the working class.

baklava [bach-LAV-a] This Greek dessert tastes like it should be loaded with calories—and it is. It's made of phyllo dough laced with pure butter, drenched in honey, and topped with nuts. Off our list.

ballotine [bahl-low-TEEN] A bundled fish (as in boned, rolled, and tied with string) that's been roasted. Don't confuse with GALANTINE, which is fish that has been tied up and poached.

balsamic vinegar [bahl-SAM-ic] The newest "in" salad dressing. Made from the juice of white Trebbiano grapes, it gets its dark color and wonderful flavor from aging in wood casks. It contains no fat and almost no calories. Those Italians think of everything.

bauerwurst [BOW-er-verst] A rather coarse German sausage that's both smoked and highly seasoned—two items which would put it off your menu even if it weren't full of fat (which it is).

bean curd Not as bad as it sounds, the humble bean curd is actually tofu, which is made from curdled milk taken from ground soybeans. It's high in calcium, low in fat, and can be flavored to taste like just about anything from cheese to meat.

béarnaise sauce [ber-NAYZ] Served on meat, fish, and vegetables, this sauce is a combination of butter and egg yolks which have been combined with vinegar, wine, tarragon, and shallots. Yummy and only for special occasions.

béchamel sauce [bay-sha-MEL] A rich sauce base made from butter, flour, and milk. If it's on your food, get out the calorie counter.

beefalo [BEEF-a-lo] Cross a buffalo with a cow, and you get beefalo. This cow-like critter produces a very lean meat with a stronger flavor than beef. Found in many Tex-Mex restaurants.

beignet [ben-YAY] Found down New Orleans way, the beignet is a yeast pastry that's deep-fried and dusted with powdered sugar. If it wasn't so delicious, it would far easier to warn you against it.

Beluga caviar [buh-LOO-guh KA-vee-ahr] Caviar, of course, is lightly salted fish eggs. Beluga caviar is the very best kind, harvested from the Caspian sea. Of the varying kinds of beluga, the finest is called the Shah's Golden. Eat it on someone else's tab. Do not confuse with "lumpfish caviar," which is what you get on airplanes.

bergamot [BER-gah-mot] The peel of this small, potent orange is traditionally put in EARL GREY TEA. You'll also find it candied or extracted as a scent in perfume.

beurre [burr-r] Butter, *en français*.

Bibb lettuce Also called butterhead or limestone lettuce, this vegetable has soft, tender, and quite sweet leaves for use in the best salads. Don't just save it for company. Enjoy often.

billi-bi [billy-BEE] A rich, rich soup made from cream, wine, onions, and mussels that is often found on menus in French restaurants. One taste is enough to send you back to the treadmill.

biscotto [bee-SCOT-toh] A twice-baked Italian cookie that is usually served in coffee houses for dipping in your favorite blend. Very crunchy and not that overwhelmingly fattening, so indulge.

blini [BLEE-knee] A small (but fattening) buckwheat pancake which is typically served with sour cream and caviar or smoked salmon. The blini originated with the czars of Russia.

blintz [BLIHNTS] You haven't lived until you've tasted this ultra-thin pancake that's rolled and then filled with ricotta cheese or other delicacy. On second thought, just take my word for it.

boeuf bourguignon [BEUF boor-gee-NYON] Tender beef that has been braised in red wine and garnished with tiny white onions or mushrooms. Delicious.

bok choy [bahk CHOY] Looking like fat, white celery, this vegetable is sometimes mislabeled Chinese cabbage. It finds its way into a lot of oriental dishes, but is nutritious to eat by itself anytime.

borscht [BOHR-sh] A low-cal soup made from beets. It came to the United States by way of Poland and Russia, and along the way, vegetables and meat were added. Stick with the original.

bouillabaisse [BOOL-yuh-BAYZ] A seafood stew in which the ingredients are open to discussion, but always heavy in garlic. The end result is typically ladled over thick French bread.

bruschetta [broo-SKET-ta] A potent garlic bread that's been drizzled with olive oil and coated in salt and pepper.

bubble and squeak The British name for mashed potatoes and cabbage. The name is said to come from the sound your stomach makes after eating the dish.

buñuelo [boo-NWAY-low] It's a metico pastry; it's deep-fried; and it's full of sugar.

butternut squash Big (often a foot long) and fat (between 3 and 5 inches), this yellow-orange squash is delicious when baked or steamed and is a treat available year-round.

C

cacciatore [catch-a-TOR-ee] Anything made with tomatoes, onions, mushrooms, and wine. Most often linked with chicken, cacciatore is the Italian word for "hunter."

caldo verde [KALD-o VAIR-dee] A wonderful soup from Portugal (caldo verde means green soup to the locals) in which potatoes and diced KALE are mixed with sausage pan-fried in olive oil. Incredibly delicious, but watch your intake.

calf's-foot jelly I would love to find out who first came up with the concept of boiling calf's feet until they release a natural gelatin, which in turn is refrigerated with lemon juice and wine until set. Go figure.

calzone [cal-ZONE-nay]   A giant pizza masquerading as a turnover. Look for calzones that are brushed with olive oil and baked, rather than deep fried.

capers [KAY-pers]   This vegetable garnish is actually the bud of a rather ugly bush native to the Mediterranean. Since the tiny caper is typically cured in salt and vinegar, it is best to rinse them well before using.

cappelletti [cap-a-LET-tee]   Think of cappelletti as tiny raviolis and you've got the point. Usually, though not always, the pasta squares are filled with meat.

carambola [care-em-BOHL-a]   This delicious golden yellow fruit is also called star fruit for its distinctive star shape when cut crosswise. Its crunchy tart and sweet flavor is only accentuated when you eat the peel.

carpaccio [car-PAH-chee-oh]   Another one of those seemingly harmless Italian appetizers that's just loaded with fat and salt . In this case, combine shaved beef fillet with olive oil, lemon juice, and mayonnaise; then top it all with CAPERS.

cassata [ca-SAAT-a]   Translated from the Italian, cassata means "in a chest," which is exactly what you'll be grabbing if you eat this dessert which contains RICOTTA cheese, candied fruit, and grated chocolate.

cassis [kah-SEES]   A sweet liqueur made from European black currants, which when added to champagne becomes a Kir Royale.

celeriac [cell-LER-ee-ack]   One of the ugliest vegetables you can imagine, this root tastes a little like strong celery. Despite its appearance, it's full of goodness including vitamin B, calcium, and iron.

cèpes [SEHP]   A rare wild mushroom with a meaty texture and wonderful woody taste, cèpes are called *porcini* in Italy and *steinpilze* in Germany. Delicious.

chantilly [shan-TIL-ee]   Danger. Anything that includes the word "chantilly" is heaped with whipped cream. Look but don't taste.

chorizo [chor-EE-zo]   Hot and spicy, this coarsely textured pork sausage is found in many Mexican and Spanish cooking.

chow-chow A vegetable relish which is said to have been brought to America by Chinese railroad workers. Chow-chow has a mustard base.

colcannon [kul-CAN-non] Thank the Irish peasants for this mashed potato dish in which milk and butter are blended with onions and kale.

conchiglie [kon-KEE-lie] A tiny seashell-shaped pasta that's more fun than practical.

coriander [KOR-ee-an-der] An aromatic fruity herb ripened and dried. Used to flavor pickles, curries, confectioneries, and liquors.

corn pone [pohn] An eggless version of cornbread which is typically shaped in tiny ovals and deep fried.

cotechino [coh-ta-KEE-no] A thick, long pork sausage that is seasoned with nutmeg and white pepper. A Northern Italian specialty.

crespelle [krehs-PELL-ay] A very thin pancake which the Italians love to stack and fill with layers of jelly or syrup.

croustade [crew-STAAD] The edible bowl in which stew or thick vegetable soups are served. Normally made of a thick pastry or bread, the croustade should be baked or deep fried before filling to keep what's inside from leaking outside.

cuisine minceur [quee-ZEEN man-SEUR] A type of cooking hallmarked by low-fat and no cream developed by French gourmet chef Michel Guerard in the mid 1970s.

cuttlefish A tender version of squid or octopus, this tentacled fish is served in Japanese and Indian restaurants.

D

daikon [DI-khon] You haven't seen a radish until you've seen a daikon. This Japanese root is excellent shredded in salads, or cut up and eaten as part of a stir-fry. Low in calories, high in taste.

deep-fry Just a reminder: Don't!

devils on horseback Toast points which are topped by oysters and a chili pepper, then wrapped in bacon. If you're really a little devil, try adding a dash of Tabasco sauce.

diable sauce [dee-AH-ble #505] A spirited accompaniment for meat or poultry which combines wine, vinegar, shallots, and abundant black pepper.

Dijon mustard [dee-JAAN] Long before Grey Poupon™ made this mustard a favorite in American kitchens, it was the hallmark of the French town of Dijon. Expect the flavor to be slightly hot, always sharp, and eternally delicious. Works on everything from sandwiches to fish.

dill Easy to grow in your home garden, dill stands as the tallest herb (at three feet). Even if you can't cultivate it yourself, always try for the freshest possible, and never use the dried variety. It adds nothing but expense.

dim sum The original "one from column A; two from column B" Chinese snacks are normally ordered individually and priced by counting the empty plates. Dim sum can contain anything—and usually does. The assortment can be tempting, so choose only those that have been steamed and remember to limit your intake.

ditalini [deet-ah-LEE-nee] The tiniest and shortest of the macaroni tubes.

dollop [DOLL-up] A giant spoonful of whipped cream, as in a "dollop of chantilly," and in "don't-you-dare."

dragée [dra-ZHAY] Those hard, tiny candies which are scattered on cookies and icings.

duchess potatoes Cholesterol city disguised as potatoes mixed with egg yolks and butter and piped into cute little mounds.

duck sauce There's no duck in duck sauce; it's called that because you serve it with duck. The concoction includes puréed plums, apricots, spices, and a gob of sugar. Sometimes hides under the name "plum sauce" for reasons that are now obvious.

durian [DOOR-ee-ann] Weighing in at over ten pounds, this giant fruit from Malaysia is covered in thick spikes. It looks disgusting and smells even worse. The flesh is considered a delicacy in Asia.

duxelles [doo-ZEL-] A paste created by the combining of finely chopped shallots, mushrooms, and herbs, then cooked in butter.

E

Earl Grey tea Named for Charles, the second Earl of Grey, this popular black tea is a favorite with the ladies who lunch.

Edam cheese [EE-dahm] This light cheese from Holland normally comes wrapped in red paraffin. Because of its high skim milk content, it is slightly lower in fat than other cheeses and is an excellent selection if the Star Dieter must snack on a slim slice of cheese. Remember, though, that *any* cheese is a detour down a closed road on this diet— even Edam.

elderberry A dark purple berry that grows on the elder tree, the elderberry is excellent in pies and was a staple for hooch made in rural stills. Rarely seen in supermarkets, the elderberry is the stuff of specialty stores.

Emmentaler cheese [Em-en-tall-er] The most famous cheese exported from Switzerland, it's the one with the holes and is normally called Swiss cheese. Yes, it goes great in a sandwich with baked ham. No, you can't eat it.

empanada [EM-pan-a-da] This stuffed turnover pastry is a a favorite in Argentina, Brazil, Spain, and Mexico. Stuffed with meat when served as an entrée, empanadas may also be filled with fruit or vegetables.

endive [ENN-dive] A type of green that is used in both salads and main courses, endive has a sharp taste which becomes bitter with age, making it imperative to use only the freshest leaves. ESCAROLE is a type of endive.

enokitake mushroom [en-oh-key-TA-key] These super-skinny, tiny-capped mushrooms grow in clumps and are sold the same way. They have a wonderful, crunchy taste, and are perfect raw in salads.

entrecôte [en-tray-COAT] The French have a way of finding fabulous things. One of them is this tender cut of beef extracted from between the ninth and eleventh ribs of a young cow.

epazote [eh-pa-ZO-tee] One of those herbs that can easily ruin a recipe if you use a heavy hand, epazote tastes like strong coriander herb.

escabéche [es-ka-BEESCH] Spanish for a poached fish that is typically topped with a special hot marinade and refrigerated. Usually served as an appetizer or in small portions, owing to its spicy afterkick.

escarole [EHS-ka-roll] A type of ENDIVE, escarole has a milder flavor, and is popular for salads and soups. It is distinguished by its broad, curved leaves.

espresso [es-PRESS-o] A strong, flavorful Italian coffee that is the darker brother of CAPPUCCINO. Available in a decaf version for the meek at heart.

Explorateur cheese [ex-PLOR-a-tor] One of the fattiest cheeses from France, Explorateur is so rich that it normally turns up as a dessert offered with a dry white wine. Look but don't touch.

F

fagioli [fa-ZHEE-o-lee] Fagioli simply means "beans" in Italian. In the United States, fagioli are typically white kidney beans.

fajitas [fa-HEE-tas] Marinated meat cut into strips that is coupled with julienned vegetables and served on a red-hot skillet in Mexican restaurants. The ingredients are rolled in a tortilla before eating. Enjoy your fajitas without the guacamole which normally comes as a sauce.

fava bean The most unattractive of the bean family, this flat, large, tan bean looks like a lima with a thyroid problem. Used in many Mideastern dishes, I think the fava is an acquired taste.

feijoa [fay-YOH-ah] Sometimes referred to as pineapple guava in the supermarkets, the feijoa is a small, egg-shaped fruit with an incredibly sweet center that is a delicious surprise in fruit salads.

fennel [FEN-uhl] Each part of this plant is edible (except the roots). The oval seeds from the green fennel plant are an excellent herb when ground and added to dishes. The pale green stems look somewhat like fat celery and have a wonderfully light, slightly licorice flavor. Fennel greens are perfect to add as a low-cal, last-minute flavor enhancer to soups and sauces.

fettucini[fet-tuh-CHEEN-ee]   A form of pasta which is flat and narrow. Think LINGUINE, only slimmer.

flageolet [fla-zho-LAY]   This wonderful and tender French kidney bean has such a special, delicate flavor you won't want to camouflage it in heavy sauces or spices. High in protein, nutrients, and flavor.

flan   A custard which usually has a caramel topping that is popular in Spanish-speaking countries. Flan is a rich dessert which is best shared by the entire table. Yes, you can taste (just use a small spoon).

Florentine [FLOR-en-teen]   A dish prepared "Florentine" is done in the style of Florence, Italy. Usually, what will arrive at your plate is a piece of fish on a bed of spinach. At all costs avoid the sauce that comes hand-in-glove with Florentine. It's called Mornay, and is heavy in fat and cheese.

focaccia [fo-CAATCH-e-ah]   A flat Italian bread that is drizzled with olive oil, garlic, and salt. Think of it as pizza without the cheese and sauce.

foie gras [FWAH GRAH]   If the liver of a goose that has been forced-fed fat for six months is appealing to you, here's a word of advice: The fat that went into the goose liver is still there. That's the real reason it's so delicious.

farfalle[far-FALL-ee]   Pasta shaped like mini bows.

frittata [free-TAHT-ta]   The Italian version of an omelet, though it's never folded like its American cousin. Instead, the frittata is served flat with various vegetables and meats mixed right in.

fusilli [foo-SEE-lee]   Think spiraled pasta cut to spoon-size lengths of about 2 inches, and you've got fusilli.

G

Gado gado [GAH-dough GAH-dough]   The spicy peanut sauce which accompanies this Indonesian dish of barely cooked vegetables is thick with coconut milk. High in fat; high in taste.

galantine [GAL-un-teen]   What could the French have been thinking when they wrapped an organ PÂTÉ with cold meat or poultry. Probably the legions of fans who love to serve this rich dish on special occasions.

ganache [gahn-NASH]   Picture chocolate whipped cream served warm and you've got the feel of ganache.

garbanzo bean [Gar-BAHN-zo]   Found throughout the Mediterranean, the garbanzo bean is a legume which finds its way into many a salad, and is ground to a paste to make HUMMUS. The Mexicans have also adopted this highly nutritious bean as a staple of their diet.

gazpacho [gaz-PAH-cho]   A wonderful Spanish soup made from a puree of fresh vegetables and served cold and crisp. Skip the crouton garnish and eat, eat, eat!

gelato [jel-LAH-toe]   Italian for "yum."—actually, it's Italian for ice cream and is quite a bit more fattening than its American sister.

génoise [jen-WAHZ]   The lightest of sponge cakes made with flour, sugar, butter, eggs, and vanilla. Commonly used as the thin base for rolled ice cream cake, the génoise is delicious as a taste treat. Do not eat the whole cake!

gnocchi [NO-kee]   Italian for "dumpling," gnocchi are made from potatoes and, on its own, is very healthy and dietetic. Unfortunately, tradition dictates that it be served with a creamy cheese or red sauce. Keep the gnocchi, lose the cream.

Gorgonzola [gore-gohn-ZOL-ah]   Together with PARMESAN, the greatest cheeses of Italy. Gorgonzola is often misnamed "blue cheese" by the uninitiated, who spot the bluish-green veins which run through this delicacy. Very pungent, little Gorgonzola goes a long way, and is worth it.

Gouda [GOO-da]   Gouda is a mainstay in Holland. The tiny holes found throughout the cheese make some refer to it as "Baby Swiss."

Gruyére [groo-YAIR]   From the Swiss valley which gives it its name, Gruyére is a nutty-flavored cheese that is wonderful when eaten out-of-hand. Made in 100-pound wheels, real Gruyére is always sold in fresh-cut wedges.

guacamole [gwah-ka-MOLE-ee]   To the less Mexican among us, it's avocado dip. Venture South of the border and it becomes an institution with as many variations as chefs. In any incarnation, however, it is heavy in fat and tropical oils.

guava [GWAH-vah]   A reddish-purple fruit that is sometimes brought to the market in its unripened, greenish-yellow condition. Should you find these infants, allow them to ripen at room temperature until they turn dark and are soft to the touch. Then, enjoy this succulent fruit from South America and Hawaii.

H

hasenpfeffer [HAH-sin-fef-fur]   The German stew that features rabbit meat which has been marinated in wine vinegar for a period of days. It's no wonder they lost the war.

hearts of palm   The innermost section of the buds of the cabbage palm, the state tree of Florida. This delicacy is available canned in most places and makes a wonderful, asparagus-like addition to salads.

hoagie [HOH-gy]   A thick sandwich made on a long French roll which combines various meats, cheeses, lettuce, and tomato.

hoisin sauce [HOY-sin]   A tangy sauce used in Chinese cooking that's concocted from soybeans, garlic, chili, and salt. Commercially prepared varieties that are found in supermarkets have a high concentration of sugar.

hollandaise sauce [HOL-un-daze]   A rich, fattening, and oh-so-delicious sauce which is lavishly poured on vegetables. It's buttercream-and-egg-yolk base make it off limits, now and forever.

hominy [HAHM-i-nee]   The grain of white or yellow corn with the hull and germ removed. Hominy is a popular Southern side dish, y'all.

horehound   Despite its rather suggestive name, the horehound is a simple mint plant, distinguished by its bitter after-taste. A hard candy bears its name.

hummus [HOOM-mus] A wonderfully tempting Middle Eastern dish made from crushed garbanzo beans, lemon juice, garlic, and olive oil. While zestful Greeks scoop it up with their fingers; the more restrained among us use toasted PITA bread.

hyssop [HIS-sup] Most famous as the principle flavoring of Chartreuse liqueur, hyssop is a member of the mint family with dark green leaves and an intense, bitter flavor.

I

iceberg The most common type of lettuce, iceberg is also the least nutritious of the group. Credit its high percentage of water.

insalata [in-sah-LAH-ta] When in Italy, think salad.

Irish moss A rather ugly seaweed which grows along the coast of Ireland and in the Northeast region of the United States. When processed, Irish moss becomes carrageen, a thickening agent found in many ice creams, cosmetics, and soups.

Italian parsley The stronger-flavored sister of the popular curly parsley that adorns serving platters the world over, Italian parsley is an aggressive herb when used to flavor sauces and soups. Also called flatleaf parsley.

J

jaggery [JAG-ur-ee] A form of unrefined sugar popular throughout India, jaggery is made from the sap of indigenous palm trees. When processed into a soft spread, it makes the most delicious topping for bread and muffins.

jambalaya [jum-buh-LIE-ya] A staple of Creole cooking, jambalaya is a stew made with rice, tomatoes, onions, green peppers, and typically ham or sausage. A healthy and tasty dish if made without the meat.

Jarlsberg cheese [YAR-alz-berg] An exquisitely light and holey Swiss cheese made in the valleys of Norway.

Jerusalem artichoke When is an artichoke not an artichoke? When it's a Jerusalem artichoke. It *really* is a lumpy variety of sunflower, which is why markets sometimes label it "sunchoke." Call it what you will, this vegetable is low in calories and nutty in flavor when boiled or steamed and can be served in place of potatoes.

jícama [HICK-a-mah]   Poor misunderstood jícama. Hailing from Mexico, where its popularity is far-reaching, this vegetable resembles a potato and tastes even milder. Served raw or lightly steamed, it's a wonderful source of vitamin C.

John Dory   Named for an English fishing captain, the John Dory is a large, flat, white fish with a delicate flavor that's enhanced with gentle poaching or grilling.

julienne [joo-ley-En]   Any fruit or vegetable that is cut in thin, long, strips about the size of a McDonald's french fry.

K

kale   A wonderfully fragrant and nutritious type of cabbage, kale's rich color and frilly leaves make it an excellent addition to salads, or steamed like spinach.

katsuobushi [KAH-tsuh-oh-boo-shee]   The light pink flesh of the bonito tuna when ground, flaked, shaved-WHAT: which is a popular garnish in Japanese cooking.

kielbasa [keel-BAH-sah]   Sometimes called Polish sausage, kielbasa is a thick, smoked and spicy sausage that is useful in any ethnic dish. Unfortunately, traditional kielbasa is made from pork and its fat content is extraordinary.

kishke [KISH-ka]   A sausage made from matzo meal, onions, flour, meat, and—like most things Jewish—fat that's stuffed into an intestine. Now you know why they created Alka-Seltzer.

knaidel [ke-NAYD-le]   By any other name, the wonderful matzo ball. I make the best in the world using matzo meal, eggs, and seasoning. (Tradition calls for a healthy scoop of chicken fat in the mix as well but I've never been very traditional.)

Kobe beef [KOH-bee]   An extremely expensive type of beef which comes from Japan. The cows are bred specially, massaged with sake, and fed grain saturated with beer. Imagine what *that* does to the beef (not to mention the cow).

kohlrabi [kohl-ROB-bee]   Sometimes called a Chinese turnip, kohl-rabi has a pale purple color and a very mild flavor. When selecting kohlrabi from the market, avoid those that have soft spots (which indicate age and overripeness).

kreplach [KREP-lackh]   Not to be confused with *won ton,* this meat- or cheese-stuffed Jewish noodle dumpling is finding its way into restaurants far and wide as an accompaniment to soup.

kumquat [CUHM-kwhat]   The smallest fruit in the citrus family, the tiny orange kumquat has a sweet rind, but tart pulp. Only for the brave or particularly artistic.

L

lahvosh [lah-VOHSH]   It's thin, it's crisp, and it's dietetic when eaten in small quantities. That's the challenge. These crackers from the Middle East are that good.

lard   Fat, fat, fat . . . in this case, from pigs. While almost never used for frying or baking any longer in America, it's still the mainstay in South America and European kitchens, where the concept of low-cholesterol has yet to hit home.

latke [LAHT-kah]   A potato pancake made with onions and eggs that's all the rage at Hanukkah. Look for those that are crisp on the outside and thin as can be, and even then don't eat them.

leek   Resembling a giant scallion, the leek has a taste like an extremely mild onion.

legume [Lay-GOO-m]   High in protein, the legume is a family of vegetables that include peas, beans, lentils, and peanuts. With the exception of the soybean and peanut, all legumes are naturally low in fat.

limestone   A type of leaf lettuce (sometimes called Bibb in markets) which has small, round, buttery-textured leaves. A wonderful addition to any salad.

linguine [lin-GWEE-knee] A long, flat pasta noodle, linguine means "little tongue" in Italian.

linzertorte [LYN-zer-tort] This Austria dessert treat is made from ground almonds, spread between a buttery crust which is splashed with lemon juice and filled with raspberry jam. As lovely to look at as it is to eat.

loganberry A incredibly juicy version of the traditional blackberry, the loganberry has been baked into pies and muffins for centuries. It was also President Kennedy's favorite jam.

loquat [LOW-quat] While many markets have taken to labeling this fruit a Japanese plum, the loquat is actually closer to a pear in taste and shape, and an apricot in color. A plum it's not.

lovage [LOVE-ejeh] The French have a way of idolizing lovage like no other. This yard-long celery-like vegetable is rumored to have aphrodisiac properties. While I can't attest to that, I do know that it is low-cal, low-fat, and rather tasteless, especially when steamed.

luau [LOU-ow] The Hawaiian version of smorgasbord, a luau is an eat-till-you-drop orgy of delicacies, centered around a roast pig (complete with head).

lychee [lee-chee] Sweet Chinese fruit, nut-shaped, commonly served as dessert in Chinese restaurants.

M

mace A spice which comes from the red membrane which covers nutmeg and from which it gets its pungent flavor.

madeleine [MAD-a-lane] It was of this small, spongy dessert that Marcel Proust wrote, "I raised to my lips a spoonful of cake; a shudder ran through my whole body and I stopped, intent upon the extraordinary changes that were taking place." I feel exactly the same.

mafalda [mal-FAL-dah] Slightly narrower than a lasagna noodle, this pasta is nevertheless broad with rippled edges.

manicotti [man-a-COT-tea] A tubular pasta about 4 inches long and an inch in diameter. The size is perfect for stuffing, which most restaurants do with cheese and meat.

marjoram [MAHR-jor-uhm]   With a flavor like mild oregano and an essence that's slightly minty, marjoram is a delicate herb which is used to flavor veal and lamb.

Melba toast   Named after famed operatic diva Dame Nellie Melba, this thin, dry toast was created by French chef Auguste Escoffier to accompany soup. We use it today as a Star Diet snack.

Milanaise [mee-lan-NAISE]   Whenever something is served "Milanaise," look for breading, frying, and a lot of fat.

mirabelle [meer-a-BELL]   Sometimes called cherry plums, this fruit from Great Britain is normally deep red in color with a sweet pulp which is excellent when transformed into preserves.

mostaccioli [mos-tah-chee-OH-lee]   A 2-inch long, rather thick macaroni tube which is normally ridged to catch the thinner sauces which typically accompany it.

Mouli [MOO-lee]   A famous grater designed in France and used for cheeses, nuts, and chocolate. The Mouli has a crank which, when turned, produces an abundance of shredded delights.

moussaka [moo-sock-AH]   A Greek entrée which layers sliced eggplant and ground lamb or beef with a cheese and egg sauce. Fattening as sin.

mozzarella [maht-suh-REL-lah]   The stringy cheese on pizza. Originally produced in Italy as a bread spread, it now has been transformed into the stuff which anchors pepperoni and sausage on Domino's Dominator. A nasty way to go.

N

Neufchâtel cheese [NOO-shuh-tell]   The low-cal version of cream cheese, Neufchâtel drops the count with a reduced level of butterfat.

niçoise [knee-SWAHZ]   A salad prepared "in the style of Nice" typically using chunks of tuna, plus hard-boiled eggs, onions, green beans, and lettuce.

nockerl [KNOCK-earl]   An Austrian version of the dumpling which is dropped like so much lead in soups and stews.

nopales [no-PAH-lays] The flat paddles of the Mexican nopal cactus which are peeled, julienned, and added to salads.

nori [NO-ree] Sheets of seaweed which are wrapped around sushi and other Japanese rolls. The darker the color, the sweeter the nori, which is called *ajijsuke-nori* when brushed with soy sauce.

O

okra [OH-krah] With the oval green okra pods, you get a double treat. Not only is the vegetable rich in vitamins A and C, when cooked, okra also thickens any broth, making it perfect for soups, stews, and gumbos.

orange roughy Neither orange, nor rough, the orange roughy is a low-fat and mild-tasting fish which is a complement to any Star Diet when poached, broiled, or grilled.

orzo [OHR-zo] This tiny pasta looks like a large piece of rice. In fact, in many Italian dishes, it's the perfect rice substitute.

osso buco [OH-soh-BOO-koh] When veal shanks join olive oil, white wine, onions, tomatoes, garlic, anchovies, carrots, celery, and lemon peel, they form osso buco, an Italian favorite.

P

paella [pie-AY-yuh] A Spanish classic dish that mixes a variety of shellfish, meats, garlic, onions, peas, and tomatoes.

palm oil We list palm oil in our funny foods section to remind you that it is totally off limits for Star Dieters. Although it is made from a vegetable and therefore has no cholesterol, palm oil is 78 percent saturated fat—the highest of all cooking oils. Never let it pass your lips.

papillote [pah-pee-YOTE] The name for those cute little paper frills which decorate beef and lamb rib bones. Now you know.

Parmesan cheese [PAR-mah-zahn] The hard, dry cheese which is a favorite to grate over pasta. For the very best Parmesan, look for cheese labeled Parmigiano-Reggiano, which mean is been aged for over 2 years. Then, remember to use it sparingly. All cheese is fattening, even that made from skim milk like Parmesan.

pâté [pat-TAY]   The finely ground spread made from a mixture of meats including pork, veal, liver, or ham. Typically high in fat, pâté should be eaten only as a treat. Wash it down with some excellent champagne and really celebrate.

pepper mill   In my mother's day, pepper came from a pepper shaker. No longer. Nowadays, it's very *au courant* to grind one's pepper in a mill. The very best pepper mills are adjustable for coarse to fine grind.

pesto [PESCH-to]   This uncooked sauce contains finely chopped basil and garlic along with pine nuts, Parmesan cheese, and olive oil. A fattening favorite with pasta.

phyllo [FEE-low]   The tissue-thin pastry dough which is everywhere in Greek cooking, phyllo by itself is low-cal. It gains its fat from the layer of butter that is added when it is baked into such favorites as baklava and spanakopita.

piccalilli [PICK-a-lily]   Whoa. The spices come out in this vegetable relish that's pickled within an inch of its life and cranked up with peppers, onions, zucchini, cucumber, and cauliflower.

pierogi [peer-OH-gee]   Shaped like a half-moon and made from noodles, this Polish dumpling is typically filled with pork, cottage cheese, and other things fattening.

pig's feet   Hard to believe but these are *actually* the feet from pigs. You'll often find them in stews served at parties in the deep South, where I generally am not on the guest list.

pinto bean   Spanish for "painted," this is the most popular bean around the world. Grown in the Southwest as well as Spain, Mexico, and other Spanish-speaking countries, the pinto is a low-fat, highly nutritious stable of many Mexican foods including the legendary refried beans. Caution: They "refry" the beans in lard as a rule.

pita [PEE-ta]   A flat, round bread which forms a pocket when split, the pita is ideal for sandwiches and dipping in hummus and baba ghanoush.

pizza [PEET-sa]   Yes, yes, yes, yes, yes. But only as a treat and without any meat topping or cheese.

poori [POOR-ee]   From India, poori is a thin, round, unleavened bread that is deep-fried before serving.

pot-au-feu [pot-oh-FEUH]   While the literal translation from the French is "pot on fire," in this classic meat and vegetable dish the pot is merely heated moderately to slowly cook the contents within. Think of it as French stew.

primavera [pree-ma-VAIR-ah]   Cut vegetables used to top any kind of dish. In Italian, primavera means "in the style of spring." Fresh.

pupu [POO-poo]   Think Hawaiian; think appetizer; think fattening and delicious.

Q

quenelle [kuh-KNEEL]   A lovely little dumpling filled with veal or chicken which is poached in meat or fish stock and served with a rich, creamy sauce.

quesadilla [kay-se-DEE-yah]   Take one flour tortilla, cover with an assortment of cheeses, flip in half, and bake until warm and the cheese is slightly melted. A Mexican fiesta all by itself.

quiche [KEESH]   The French are responsible for this scrumptious bit of business which starts with pastry shell and mixes eggs, cream, cheese, plus assorted vegetables or meats or fish. Don't get me started.

quince [KWINCE]   This neglected fruit is a light yellow color and tastes like a cross between an apple and a pear. Wonderful when cooked into a pie or tart, the quince is high in vitamin C.

quinoa [KEEN-wah]   Though you may not have ever seen it on the menu, the popularity of quinoa is increasing as a nutritious grain. In fact, in some circles, it is being given the kind of publicity push normally reserved for visiting monarchy. Since quinoa is higher in protein than any other grain, it deserves the advance press.

R

radicchio [rah-DEE-kee-oh] Another designer lettuce. This time it's red-leafed, Italian, and extremely popular because of its color and subtle flavor.

ramekin [RAM-a-kin] Those tiny little soufflé dishes that hold anything from baked delights to chilled deserts.

ratatouille [ra-tuh-TOO-ee] Oh-so-Italian mélange of chopped eggplant, tomatoes, garlic, zucchini, onions, and bell peppers, all simmered in olive oil until it screams perfection.

refried beans The Mexicans have a way of taking perfectly nutritious pinto beans and mashing them to death before frying them in lard. Stick with a TOSTADA.

rémoulade [ray-muh-LAHD] Combine mayonnaise, capers, mustard, and chopped gherkins and you get the French version of tartar sauce. Avoid.

ricotta [ree-COT-ta] A grainy cheese similar in appearance to cottage cheese that is a principle ingredient in LASAGNA and MANICOTTI.

risotto [ree-ZAW-toe] A wonderful rice dish from Italy that typically is floating in butter and cheese. If you can find an herb risotto without either of the latter, eat till your stomach says *graci*.

rocambole [ROCK-um-bowl] It looks like a LEEK and it tastes like mild garlic. Feel free to use it like either.

romaine [ro-MAIN] The absolutely most fabulous lettuce on earth, romaine is the primary ingredient in Caesar salad as well as many others. It's nutritious, crunchy, green and wonderful.

rugalach [RUHG-a-lahkh] Those too-easy-to-eat cookies made with cream-cheese dough, stuffed with jam or raisins and served at Hanukkah.

rutabaga [ROO-ta-beg-ah] An oversized turnip that has a pale, yellow skin and a slightly sweet taste. Low in calories, the often overlooked rutabaga is also rich in vitamin C.

S

salad spinner Still another device that was unheard of in your mother's kitchen. It whips around wet lettuce until it's dry. How did we ever do without it?

salsa [SAHL-sa] "Salsa" means sauce in Spanish, with the Mexicans turning it into a chunky, tomato-rich blend of vegetables that becomes an excellent, low-fat topping for meats, potatoes, salads, and fish.

saltimbocca [sahl-tim-BOH-ka] The leanest veal, sliced very thin and topped with prosciutto, before it's sautéd in butter and a splash of white wine. How do the Italians do it?

Santa Claus melon So named because of its yellow and green skin, you might mistake this melon for a watermelon if it weren't for its bright yellow flesh. Also called Christmas melon because that's when this fruit is in season.

sashimi [sah-SHEE-me] Raw fish that is served with WASABI and soy sauce, and is commonly confused with SUSHI by most novitiates.

semolina [sem-oh-LEAN-a] The stuff that makes the best pasta, semolina is coarsely ground durum wheat. Nothing more.

shiitake [shee-TAH-key] A large, dark brown mushroom that is known for both its flavor and medicinal qualities. While the taste is quite tangy, the real secret that the shiitake holds is its claim to pump up the human immune system.

soba [SOH-ba] A Japanese noodle that's made from buckwheat flour and has a wicked aftertaste.

sopaipilla [soh-py-PEE-ya] Commonly called the national dessert of Mexico, this puffy, air-filled pastry was actually created in New Mexico. No matter the origin, it's popular on both sides of the border and in either place it's just as fattening.

sorbet [sore-BAY] The difference between sherbet and sorbet is that, while both are fruit ices, the sorbet is never made with cream. You can't say the same for sherbet.

spanakopita [span-a-KOH-pee-ta]   Very addicting, very caloric Greek version of spinach pie. The spinach part is great. It's all the feta cheese they interlace plus the butter-drenched PHYLLO dough that causes the commotion and the concern.

suet [SUE-it]   The disgusting white fat found in beef and lamb. Better to save it for candles than to eat it in pastries and mincemeat pie.

sushi [SUE-she]   Boiled rice flavored with rice vinegar. Among the many varieties of sushi to be found in Japanese restaurants are those than serve it with thin slices of raw fish and/or are rolled in NORI seaweed. Not to be confused with SASHIMI.

sweetbreads   The thymus gland of young cows. Yukh!

Szechuan [SEHCH-wahn]   Hot, hot, hot Chinese food. The foundation of Szechuan cooking is the spicy Szechuan pepper which gives it its kick. Order Szechuan and ask for a fire extinguisher to go.

T

tabbouleh [ta-BOO-lee]   A refreshing Middle Eastern dish made by mixing finely chopped tomatoes, onions, parsley, and mint with bulghur wheat and olive oil.

tagliatelle [tall-ya-TELL-lee]   What you'd call FETTUCCINE in Northern Italy and thereabouts.

tahini [ta-HEE-ni]   A paste made from ground sesame seeds, tahini is a sauce used in Greek and other Middle Eastern dishes and is found in *hummus* and BABA GHANOUSH.

tapas [TOP-pas]   The Spanish rendition of PUPUS. Eat enough of these tasty and varied appetizers and they can form your entire meal.

tempura [tehm-POOR-ah]   The Japanese way to raise the calories of low-fat food. In their version, they batter and deep-fry fish and vegetables.

teriyaki [tehr-ee-YAK-ee]   A high-sodium sauce used in oriental cooking that is made of soy, sugar, ginger, and sake.

toad-in-the-hole   Leave it to the British to come up with a dish called toad-in-the-hole. Please! It's sausages wrapped in YORKSHIRE PUDDING and baked until they're puffy. Toad-in-the-hole, indeed.

tostada [toast-STAD-a]   Deep-fry a tortilla and fill or top it with REFRIED BEANS, tomatoes, lettuce, cheese, and such super-fattening additions such as GUACAMOLE and sour cream.

truffle [TRUHF-ahl]   A fungus which is practically worshipped around the world. It certainly isn't for its appearance, which is wrinkled, thick, and positively ugly. Thin slices of the expensive truffle are added to pasta and cheese dishes as well as a variety of main courses. No one mentions that specially trained pigs unearth these pungent fungi.

truffle [TRUHF-ahl]   No, you're not seeing double. This truffle is the chocolate kind, sometimes shaped to resemble the round, ugly truffle above. The chocolate truffle is thick with butter, sugar, flavor, and calories.

U

ugli [UGLY]   This grapefruit-like fruit is from Jamaica and adds traces of orange or tangerine flavor to the normally tart grapefruit pulp. A treat when you can find it (and it's anything but ugly).

V

vermicelli [ver-ma-CHEL-lee]   In Italian, *vermicelli* means "little worms," an unfortunate vision when you realize how delicious this thin spaghetti pasta really is.

vichyssoise [vihsh-she-SWAHZ]   A cold, potato-and-LEEK soup that's typically garnished with chopped chives for color.

W

wasabi [wah-SAAB-bee]   Green in color, and powerful in flavor, wasabi is the Japanese version of horseradish. Hot stuff.

wild rice   This long grain comes from the marsh grass of the Great Lakes area and really isn't a rice at all. It's nutty flavor and crunchy texture complement many a stuffing, and it is particular popular when served with Cornish game hen or other poultry.

won ton [WAHN-tahn] A thin-skinned version of RAVIOLI, won ton is a staple of Chinese cooking. You'll find it in soups, served deep-fried for dipping, or steamed as an appetizer. A larger version of the skins are used to wrap egg rolls.

X

xanthan gum [ZAN-thun] This food thickener and emulsifier is made from fermented sugar. You'll find it listed as in ingredient in many commercially prepared salad dressings.

Xuzhou [sue-JOE] A type of Chinese cooking using light broths and raw vegetables named for the city in the Northwest Jiangu province.

Y

yakitori [yak-ee-TOE-ree] From the Japanese words *yaki* (grilled) and *tori* (fowl), yakitori now refers to skewered and grilled chicken topped with a marinade of TERIYAKI.

Yorkshire pudding [YORK-sheer] Though having nothing to do with a traditional pudding, this side dish is served with beef in whose drippings it is baked. Named for a town in England, the Yorkshire pudding contains eggs, flour, and milk and puffs up like a soufflé.

Z

zabaglione [zah-bah-YOH-nay] When it comes to desserts, the Italians are on par with the French. In this incredible creation, the Italians combine egg yolks, Marsala wine, and sugar and whip it into a custard that defies description. P.S. The French stole the recipe and called it *sabayon.*

ziti [ZEE-tee] A long, thin tube of macaroni pasta, the ziti is traditionally complemented with marinara sauce.

zuccotto [zoo-COT-to] Still another wonderful Italian dessert, this one is made with whipped cream, grated chocolate, and chopped nuts, all circled by liqueur-drenched cake.

APPENDIX IV

Metric Conversion Charts

Roger Karnbad

With Oscar De La Hoya at the grand opening of his gym in L.A.

Formulas for conversion

Fahrenheit to Celsius: subtract 32, multiply by 5, then divide by 9
for example:

$$212°F - 32 = 180$$
$$180 \times 5 = 900$$
$$900 \div 9 = 100°C$$

Celsius to Fahrenheit: multiply by 9, the divide by 5, then add 32
for example:

$$100°C \times 9 = 900$$
$$900 \div 5 = 180$$
$$180 + 32 = 212°F$$

Temperatures (Fahrenheit to Celsius)

−10°F =	−23°C	coldest part of freezer
0°F =	−17°C	freezer
32°F =	0°C	water freezes
68°F =	20°C	room temperature
85°F =	29°C	
100°F =	38°C	
115°F =	46°C	water simmers
135°F =	57°C	water scalds
140°F =	60°C	
150°F =	66°C	

160°F = 71°C
170°F = 77°C
180°F = 82°C   water simmers
190°F = 88°C
200°F = 95°C
205°F = 96°C   water simmers
212°F = 100°C   water boils, at sea level
225°F = 110°C
250°F = 120°C   very low (or slow) oven
275°F = 135°C   very low (or slow) oven
300°F = 150°C   low (or slow) oven
325°F = 165°C   low (or moderately slow) oven
350°F = 180°C   moderate oven
375°F = 190°C   moderate (or moderately hot) oven
400°F = 205°C   hot oven
425°F = 220°C   hot oven
450°F = 230°C   very hot oven
475°F = 245°C   very hot oven
500°F = 260°C   extremely hot oven/broiling
525°F = 275°C   extremely hot oven/broiling

LIQUID MEASURES CONVERSION

For foods such as yogurt, applesauce, or cottage cheese that are not quite liquid, but not quite solid, use fluid measures for conversion.

Both systems, the US Standard and Metric, use spoon measures. The sizes are slightly different, but the difference is not significant in general cooking (It may, however, be significant in baking.)

Tbs = tablespoon   teas = teaspoon

Spoons, cups, pints, quarts	Fluid oz	Milliliters (ml), deciliters (dl) and liters (l); rounded off
1 teaspoon (tsp)	⅙ oz	5 ml
3 tsp (1 Tbs)	½ oz	15 ml

1 Tbs	1 oz	¼ dl (or 1 Tbs)
4 Tbs (¼ c)	2 oz	½ dl (or 4 Tbs)
⅓ c	2⅔ oz	¾ dl
½ c	4 oz	1 dl
¾ c	6 oz	1¾ dl
1 c	8 oz	250 ml (or ¼ L)
2 c (1 pint)	16 oz	500 ml (or ½ L)
4 c (1 quart)	32 oz	1 L
4 qt (1 gallon)	128 oz	3¾ L

Solid Measures Conversion

Converting solid measures between US standard and metrics is not as straightforward as it might seem. The density of the substance being measured makes a big difference in the volume to weight conversion. For example, 1 tablespoon of flour is ¼ ounce and 8.75 grams whereas 1 tablespoon of butter or shortening is ½ ounce and 15 grams. The following chart is intended as a guide only, some experimentation may be necessary to achieve success.

Formulas for conversion
    ounces to grams: multiply ounces by 28.35
    grams to ounces: multiply grams figure by .035

ounces	pounds	grams	kilograms
1		30	
4	¼	115	
8	½	225	
9		250	¼
12	¾	430	
16	1	450	
18		500	½
	2¼	1000	1
	5		2¼
	10		4½

LINEAR MEASURES CONVERSION

Pan sizes are very different in countries that use metrics versus the US standard. This is more significant in baking than in general cooking.

Formulas for conversion
inches to centimeters: multiply the inch by 2.54
centimeters to inches: multiply the centimeter by 0.39

inches	cm	inches	cm
½	1½	9	23
1	2½	10	25
2	5	12 (1 ft.)	30
3	8	14	35
4	10	15	38½
5	13	16	40
6	15	18	45
7	18	20	50
8	20	24 (2 ft.)	60